Becoming an Accountant

Is accountancy really the career for you?

First edition

Edited by Stuart Chandler

FRANCIS HOLLAND SCHOOL
CAREERS

D1439629

BPP LEARNING MEDIA

First edition 2012

ISBN 9781 4453 9728 3
e-ISBN 9781 4453 9737 5

British Library Cataloguing-in-Publication Data
A catalogue record for this book is available from the British Library

Published by
BPP Learning Media Ltd
BPP House, Aldine Place
London W12 8AA

www.bpp.com/health

Printed in the United Kingdom by
Ricoh
Ricoh House
Ullswater Crescent
Coulsdon
CR5 2HR

Your learning materials, published by BPP Learning Media Ltd, are printed on paper sourced from sustainable, managed forests.

BPP
LEARNING MEDIA

Contents

Free companion material

Readers can access additional companion material for free online.

To access companion material please visit:
www.bpp.com/freehealthresources.

About the publisher

BPP Learning Media is dedicated to supporting aspiring professionals with top quality learning material. BPP Learning Media's commitment to success is shown by our record of quality, innovation and market leadership in paper-based and e-learning materials. BPP Learning Media's study materials are written by professionally-qualified specialists who know from personal experience the importance of top quality materials for success.

About the editor

Editor and lead author

Stuart Chandler ACCA

Stuart qualified as a Chartered Certified Accountant with a private bank. During his career – including audit work at a Big Four firm and fund work at an international financial services provider – he sought an active role in coaching and developing junior staff, resulting in a career as a tutor at BPP.

Stuart is committed to the cause of professional qualifications, both as an education provider and qualified accountant. He lives and works in Guernsey, Channel Islands, with his wife Rachel and bulldog Ron.

About the contributors

Chapter 3

Clare Buck ICMA

Clare qualified as a Chartered Management Accountant with Ford. She has significant experience working in industry at a senior management level.

Following her departure from industry, she joined BPP in Liverpool as a tutor, specialising in management accounting and written subjects. This led to a role as Lead Internal Verifier and Quality Assurance Director for AAT and Foundation Courses. She now heads the Vocational School, having championed Apprenticeships as an entry route in accountancy.

Chapter 5

Sadie Farrington BA (Hons) CAT ATT CTA

Sadie has a Japanese degree from Durham and is a Chartered Tax Adviser. After graduating, she worked in Japan as a translator for the Japanese government. Following this, she moved to the tax department of a Big Four firm in London. After qualifying, she relocated to the Channel Islands.

Sadie moved to BPP in 2007 and gained her CAT qualification before beginning her ACCA exams. She now lives in Yorkshire where she teaches accounting and tax in Leeds.

Chapter 4

Lucy Freckleton BA (Hons) ACA

Lucy has an Economics degree from Bath and qualified as a Chartered Accountant with a Big Four firm in their audit department. Her career includes work as a management accountant at the BBC, and a financial management role at Electronic Arts.

In 2002, Lucy moved to BPP as a tutor and has been delivering financial training courses ever since. She lives in Hampshire with her two young sons and her cross-eyed cat Minty.

Foreword

If anyone had asked me what I wanted to be when I grew up I am pretty certain I wouldn't have said 'being an accountant.' Both my parents worked for the Civil Service and their ambitions for me were to make it to an 'office job' – whatever that meant!

Looking back now, 20 years after qualifying as an accountant, I can safely say that I have had a hugely varied career thanks to the foundations that this profession has offered me in business. It has been a long time since I have worked in a finance department but the knowledge of how an organisation works from a financial perspective is hugely beneficial for anyone looking to work in any career or organisation type. When I was in my early twenties I had no clear idea of what I wanted to do, but the professional 'badge' of accountancy has enabled me to weave a career that has included client management, product development and general management of a business.

Becoming an Accountant is the sort of book every teenager, parent or career advisor should have access to – it is practical, informative and based on the real world – all the information that you need to help make informed decisions on your future career path.

At BPP Professional Education we train approximately 20,000 trainee accountants every year, from all walks of life and backgrounds. We try to make the journey through these professional exams as easy and painless as possible, but the challenge is very real and the commitment required by every trainee is very clear.

To have the resolve to see this challenge through, every trainee needs to understand both the rewards that success will bring (not just financially in the short term, but also to their overall career) as well as the hard work they must put in over a long period of time to achieve this success. It is in this area that I believe that *Becoming an Accountant* is so unique; it enables every individual to approach this career with their eyes wide open. As the saying goes 'forewarned is forearmed' and the more you enter a potential career with insight, the better it is for all involved.

Choosing a career is a key decision in your life, and one of the many great things about accountancy as a career is that it offers so much flexibility to you over the course of 20 to 30 years. My advice to you would be to read on to see whether this is a career route that meets your particular professional and personal ambitions – enjoy!

Martin Taylor ACMA
CEO
BPP Professional Education

BPP
LEARNING MEDIA

Acknowledgments

I would like to thank BPP Learning Media for the opportunity to write this book, and pursue the dream of having something published, notably Matt and Chloe for their patience and guidance.

My sincere thanks go out to Clare, Sadie and Lucy who put in huge amounts of time, effort and research for their chapters, making my job of editing that much easier!

Many thanks to everyone who agreed to review or to be quoted or 'case studied,' throughout the book, helping bring a healthy dose of reality, which is very useful for those considering entering accountancy.

Case studies and quotes are reproduced with kind permission from Amanda Bell, Naomi Nesbit, Philippa James, Sarah Pick, Steve Newberry, Sue Brown, Rachel Chandler, Sarah Edmunds, Alex Burne, Ben Carson, Sadie Farrington, Matthew Tyne and Gary Dewey.

Finally, I would like to thank BPP Professional Education Guernsey for their patience with me during writing and editing, and Rachel for always being supportive...and reviewing my final draft!

Shining a light on your future career path

The process of researching and identifying a career that you are most suited to can be a somewhat daunting process, but the rewards of following a career that truly engages you should not be underestimated. Deciding on your future career path should be viewed as a fun and extremely satisfying process that, if done correctly, will benefit you greatly.

Carefully considering a short list of future career options and what each one will offer you will help you to make a truly informed decision. Although it is perfectly acceptable to change career direction at a later date, reviewing the options open to you now will help to ensure that you are satisfied with your career from the outset.

I first began mentoring aspiring professionals eight years ago when it was clear that many individuals were not gaining access to the careers guidance they required. It was with this in mind that I embarked on publishing our *Becoming a* series of books, to provide help, support and clear insight into career choices. I hope that this book will help you to make an informed decision as to what career you are most suited to, your strengths and your aspirations.

I would like to take this opportunity to wish you the very best of luck with identifying your future career and hope that you pass on some of the gems of wisdom that you acquire along the way, to those who follow in your footsteps.

Matt Green
Series Editor – *Becoming a* series
Director of Professional Development
BPP University College of Professional Studies

Introduction

Accountants get pretty bad press, from Monty Python sailing the wide 'Accountan-sea,' to the 'Accounting Trolls' in Dilbert; the image of a calculator-toting, number-crunching and ultimately, *boring* worker has pervaded our culture for years. But don't believe everything you hear or see!

The aim of this book is to help potential employees, employers, students (whether at university or school) or those wishing to change careers understand what it is that accountants do, where they work (in terms of the location and type of work) and ultimately, how to become a qualified accountant.

Accounting Apprentice
(Reproduced with permission of Higgins Cartoons, 2012.
Originally published by Accountancy Age, 2011)

We will contemplate the qualification process for those with degrees. We will also consider the qualification process and entry routes for those who do not want to pay costly university fees but who might consider undertaking an accountancy qualification as an apprentice or school leaver (with or without academic qualifications such as GCSEs).

Over the course of this book, any myths about the stereotypical accountant will (hopefully!) be dispelled, through case studies of accountants working overseas in corporate insolvency and recovery, to those working closer to home running their own consulting firms.

With the ongoing turbulence in the global economy and subsequent birth of yet more financial jargon and buzzwords, accountants and the financial world have become more prominent, more praised, and more criticised than ever before.

Employers have had no choice but to pay greater attention to the ongoing and evolving risks of the environment in which we now live. Professional qualifications, such as those held by accountants, are a way to instantly stand out as a candidate who is committed, dedicated and hard working.

It is worth noting here, though, that the journey to becoming a qualified accountant is challenging in terms of the necessary exams and the work required. The eventual outcome is worth every second of study and overtime, as you will have a valuable skill set, leading to a well paid role; but only once you have passed the exams and obtained the relevant work experience.

Before we look into the detail of how to become an accountant, let us first consider:

What is an accountant?

An accountant should be a qualified member of a professional accounting body (such as the Institute of Chartered Accountants in Scotland or the Chartered Institute of Management Accountants). An accountant's role at its most basic is concerned with the preparation, presentation and calculation of financial information; for example, the calculation of how much tax is payable by an individual or organisation (the role of a tax accountant), or the compilation and preparation of financial records, showing what money an organisation has earned and what money it has spent (the role of a financial accountant).

Accountants also look at historic financial information and provide assurance that the information is broadly correct; this is the job of an

auditor. Bear in mind that it is not necessary to work exclusively with numbers – as we will see later in the book – accountants have the skills to do almost any kind of work!

If this has served to kindle your interest…then let us discover how you go about becoming an accountant…

Chapter 1

Overview of the accountancy industry

Stuart Chandler

Introduction

It is a commonly held perception that accountants are all expert mathematicians and that all they do is sit at a desk, working with financial information and manipulating numbers. This is not necessarily the case. In the modern working environment, you are as likely to find an accountant working in an accountancy practice as one working in the film or fashion industry.

The type of work they may undertake is vastly different, from the (albeit expected) preparation and provision of financial statements, to organising funding for a charity; the accountant's role is ever changing.

What work do accountants do?

Think of a country you would like to, or have, visited; now think of an industry within that country that you know exists; finally, think of a company within that country and industry – got one? How about Italy, the automotive industry and Ferrari? Or America, the technology industry and Apple? Any company, in almost any country, will (at some point) either use the services of, or directly employ, an accountant.

Most companies need two things to function: money and people. In order to get money from, say, a bank, the company will need information in the form of financial records indicating how they have previously earned and spent their money.

This information is compiled into financial statements; a document with reports showing how much money has been earned by, for example, selling cars (known as income) less the money spent on, say, rent, electricity and wages (known as expenses) to give a figure called profits. The income and expenses are shown in the profit & loss report (also called the income statement) in the financial statements.

These financial statements also show what the company owns, such as buildings, cash or vehicles (known as assets) less what the company owes, such as an overdraft or loans to a bank (known as liabilities) to give the net assets, or value, of the company. The assets and liabilities are shown on the balance sheet (also known as the statement of financial position) in the financial statements.

The company is not limited to asking the bank for a loan, so might choose to sell shares to people (be it family members, or members of the public) in order to inject money into the business. The shareholders then become part owners of the company, entitled to financial information regarding the company's performance.

Definition

Shares

A **share** is a unit of ownership of a company. It entitles the shareholder (sometimes referred to as a member or investor) to a share of the company's profits and losses, as well as a share of its assets and liabilities. Shareholders are allowed to attend official meetings held by the company as well as to speak at, and vote on, matters arising at these meetings.

Your desired country / industry / company combination will have used the advice of an accountant, or will employ an accountant to ensure that the financial records (think of your personal bank statement) are correct and up to date.

Accountants don't just have to work with numbers in financial statements; within the manufacturing world, they might be responsible for dealing with physical goods. A management accountant could be responsible for ordering and purchasing supplies to be processed by the production team into a final product and, in turn, the junior accountants will consider the costs and delivery logistics of these items.

Definitions

Financial versus management accountants

A **financial accountant** is responsible for recording the financial activity (ie what the organisation has earned and spent) and compiling the financial statements of an organisation. The financial statements present historic information, summarising what (and how) the company has earned (income) less what it has spent (expenses) to give profits (or possibly losses if expenses exceed income); they will also show what the company owns (assets) and deduct away what it owes (liabilities) to give the value of the company.

A financial accountant needs to have a sound understanding of the applicable laws and regulations for their organisation / industry, as well as accounting standards – such as UK Generally Accepted Accounting Practice or International Financial Reporting Standards – as the financial statements need to comply with the necessary laws, regulations and accounting standards.

A **management accountant** is responsible for analysing and presenting comprehensive internal information required by a business. Management accounts are up to date, containing highly detailed information. Management accountants are primarily concerned with costing and budgeting.

The costing side of management accounting entails establishing exactly how much it costs the business to produce one unit of a product (for example a single MP3 player) including the material used, labour time and apparently unrelated costs, such as electricity and rent (called overheads). The organisation will assess these costs and set a selling price that exceeds the total cost of the product.

The budgeting side of management accounting is concerned with estimating how much the organisation is going to earn and how much it is going to spend over the course of a year. The budget can also be used to schedule and organise the production of units. During the year, the budget is used to evaluate performance – ie how the organisation has *actually* done, compared against how it *should have* done (also known as actual v budgeted performance).

Moving outside the world revolving around numbers and financial information, accountancy training is the basis for a huge variety of jobs, whether you want to start up your own retail business or work away from the financial services or production environments. The move could entail a physical move overseas, or a horizontal move into a fundamentally different industry (for example moving from banking into hospitality).

Regardless of where you might start out, an accounting qualification provides an incredible foundation for your career, as well as a signal to prospective employers that you are dedicated, hard working and motivated enough to pass your accounting exams, which puts you in a small margin of the population who has done so.

'I wanted a qualification that was transferable, global and showed employers that I was dedicated and hard working. The Association of Chartered Certified Accountants (ACCA) qualification offered all of that.'

Where do accountants work?

Once qualified, accountants can work almost anywhere (in terms of location and industry), however the bulk of accountants tend to train and subsequently work in financial services or industry as financial practitioners. But this does not mean your career path is set in stone! There are many options for accountants, whether they want to work as a production accountant on a movie, as a construction accountant for an organisation building skyscrapers or as an energy accountant in the challenging oil and gas sector. Bear in mind that whatever you do,

you do not need to be 'just another accountant' because you happened to have trained as one; your role will develop and diversify over time, based on your particular strengths, potentially leading to a focus on business development, sales or people management to name but a few.

Each year, the Financial Reporting Council's (FRC) Professional Oversight Board produce a report detailing the *Key Facts and Trends in the Accountancy Profession* which provides comprehensive information about the number of accountants there are, where they work and which professional body they are members of. The FRC focuses on seven professional accountancy bodies ('the professional bodies'), which are outlined below:

- Association of Chartered Certified Accountants: www.accaglobal.com

- Chartered Institute of Management Accountants: www.cimaglobal.com

- Chartered Institute of Public Finance and Accountancy: www.cipfa.org.uk

- Institute of Chartered Accountants in England and Wales: www.icaew.com

- Chartered Accountants Ireland: www.charteredaccountants.ie

- Institute of Chartered Accountants in Scotland: www.icas.org.uk

- Association of International Accountants: www.aiaworldwide.com

While the scope of work that an accountant can do is only limited to your imagination, the FRC has indicated that the bulk of accountants work with facts and figures, with over 75% of the members of the professional bodies doing so.

Definition

The Financial Reporting Council

The Financial Reporting Council is the UK's independent regulator, with the aim of promoting high quality corporate governance (principles concerning how organisations are run) and reporting to encourage investment.

Part of its remit is to exercise independent oversight of the regulation of the accountancy profession by the accountancy bodies (eg ACCA or ICAEW), through the Professional Oversight Board.

Refer to Chapter 4: *Roles and specialisations in accountancy*, for more detail about what jobs accountants may do.

Case study:

Steve works for a Big Four firm in their Risk Assurance department.

Why did you choose a career in accountancy?

'I was interested in finance but it was mainly because I had done some accountancy work experience when I was at school, had enjoyed it and felt it would be a good career with a well recognised qualification.'

Why did you stay in audit after qualifying?

'I liked the idea of transitioning to manager and beyond, which meant I could lead teams and work with people (senior management at clients plus my own staff teams) which I enjoy.

The variety of work and different clients you get exposed to increases as you progress through the firm, before you then start to think about specialising. I also like the office culture and team environment which people take for granted and do not appreciate until they leave the firm.'

What do you enjoy about working in audit?

'While elements can be time pressured, there is always an end-game with a clearance meeting or a report to the client and ultimately a set of accounts with an opinion which allows a certain amount of job satisfaction when you complete an audit. Also, every client is different, with different systems, business strategies and people. Internally you get to work with a different team on each audit – there can't be that many careers or jobs where you have that variety.'

How many accountants are there?

The harsh spotlight shed on the financial industry in recent years has led regulators such as the Financial Services Authority (FSA), to mandate that certain professionals require a minimum qualification (for example those required by investment professionals under the FSA's Retail Distribution Review). However, this has always been the case in the auditing industry which constitutes a large sector of accountants in the UK.

> ## Definition
>
> ## Audit
>
> An **audit** is carried out by both trainee and qualified accountants; an audit is the independent examination of historical financial information (most commonly the annual financial statements), whereby the auditor will consider what the financial statements are stating and compare this to the underlying records, concluding by stating an opinion on the financial statements.
>
> For example the audit of cash would involve considering the cash asset on the balance sheet, and comparing this to the amount on the bank statements (and other documentation from the bank).
>
> Audit firms are external to, and independent of, the organisations they are reviewing. Auditors must be qualified accountants. See Chapter 4 for more information on auditing.

Regardless of the industry, it is considered best practice for accountants to be properly qualified (ie they have passed the necessary professional exams and have the work experience) for their roles, as the awareness of ethics, risks and legal principles is enforced throughout the exams, leading to excellent practitioners. The information from the FRC's *Key Facts and Trends in the Accountancy Profession* June 2011 report is that professional qualifications, such as those held by accountants are indeed desirable, with the awarding bodies experiencing continued growth over the past six years.

In the UK and Ireland, there are more than 304,000 qualified members of the professional bodies, representing growth of 13.9% from 2005 to 2010. Worldwide, the figures are even more impressive, with 424,000 qualified members of the professional bodies, demonstrating growth of 19.3% from 2005 to 2010, confirming that employers are keener than ever for their staff to be relevantly qualified.

The mix of accountants is also changing positively in terms of gender and age. The figures from the FRC's *Key Facts and Trends in the Accountancy Profession* June 2011 report signify this, showing a significant (and increasing) proportion of female accountants joining the professional bodies. In 2010, 34% of qualified accountants worldwide were female, showing a 5% growth since 2005.

As for younger members, qualified members aged 35 and under represented more than 100,000 or nearly 24% of qualified members worldwide. This shift is improving the reputation of the profession, as younger members embody a renewed enthusiasm and drive within the professional bodies and the broader profession.

Top tip – Developing your business skills

If you are at school or university and would like to develop your business skills further, why not join your local Young Enterprise group?

This business and enterprise education charity has been running for nearly 40 years, helping 250,000 young people learn about business and the world of work under the guidance of volunteers (who are often accountants). The most exciting opportunity is the chance to run your own company over the course of a year – what better experience is there than that?! Go to www.young-enterprise.org.uk to find your local group.

Chapter summary

An ever shifting financial landscape, coupled with a continually increasing variety and volume of work, means that accountants are more in demand – so you won't be short of work if you choose to become an accountant! Also consider that there is no longer a perception of individuals being typecast as 'just' an accountant, as their services and skills are employed by a wide range of individuals, businesses and other organisations.

Key points

- Qualified accountants are a highly desirable asset to an employer – persevere, pass your exams, work hard and you can reap the benefits.

- Most accountants start out working with financial facts and figures, choosing to explore outside of this area once they have passed their exams.

- There is no real limit on where you can work or what you can do, as many qualifications are globally recognised (see Chapter 7: *Working abroad,* for more information).

Useful resources

Financial Reporting Council: www.frc.org.uk

Financial Services Authority: www.fsa.gov.uk

Prospects (job descriptions): www.prospects.ac.uk

Young Enterprise: www.young-enterprise.org.uk

Professional accountancy bodies:

Association of Chartered Certified Accountants: www.accaglobal.com

Association of International Accountants: www.aiaworldwide.com

Chartered Accountants Ireland: www.charteredaccountants.ie

Chartered Institute of Management Accountants: www.cimaglobal.com

Chartered Institute of Public Finance and Accountancy:
www.cipfa.org.uk

Institute of Chartered Accountants in England and Wales:
www.icaew.com

Institute of Chartered Accountants in Scotland: www.icas.org.uk

References

Businessdictionary.com (2011) *What is a Share?* [Online] Available at: www.businessdictionary.com/definition/share.html [Accessed 22 November 2012].

Financial Reporting Council, Public Oversight Body (2011) – *Key Facts & Trends Reports, 2011.* [Online] Available at: www.frc.org.uk/getattachment/1b7baf93-3be3-4fba-b4c1-dec90874b23d/Key-Facts-and-Trends-in-the-Accountancy-Profession-27-June-2011.aspx [Accessed 22 November 2012].

Financial Reporting Council (2012) *About the FRC.* [Online] Available at: www.frc.org.uk/About-the-FRC.aspx [Accessed 22 November 2012].

Young Enterprise (2012) *About Us.* [Online] Available at: www.young-enterprise.org.uk/about_us [Accessed 22 November 2012].

Chapter 2

Is accountancy for you?

Stuart Chandler

Introduction

If you do some research on the internet, you will rapidly build up a picture of the skills and qualities that are, apparently, **vital** to becoming an accountant. These include: communication, patience, logic, confidence, commitment, time management, numeracy, intellect, creativity, assertiveness, ambition, reliability, organisation, integrity, initiative… and so the list continues. While there is no doubt that someone with all of those qualities would make a good accountant, they would spend so much time focusing on their qualities – rather than what they should be doing – that nothing would get done!

Desirable skills and qualities to become an accountant

With any job, qualification or employer, there is a list of desirable qualities that a trainee accountant should have. Despite the conventional view of the stereotypical, boring, colourless accountant who enjoys the manipulation of numbers, the full list of qualities is too long to be anything other than aspirational. You should therefore refer to these qualities as a guide rather than heed them too carefully.

Even if you don't feel you have all the necessary qualities to become an accountant, don't rule it out immediately – you might have exactly what it takes, but not the confidence to recognise it yet!

Qualities

Confidence and assertiveness

If, for example, you decide to train with an audit firm, it will be necessary to have 'professional scepticism' in your work (see Chapter 4 for more information on auditing), meaning that you may have to disagree with clients. Confidence will help with this, as it will in presenting and discussing financial statements to a Board of Directors.

Perseverance and tenacity

Accountancy exams are challenging and the hours of work can be long, and so elements of tenacity and perseverance will stand you in good stead. Also, consider the need to get your work done – on time and on budget – meaning these qualities will prove their worth.

Commitment and dedication

As previously explained, qualifying as an accountant will demonstrate commitment to your employer. Committing to a training contract (usually three years in length) will mean dedication to your exams and career. Bear in mind that three years out of the rest of your life is no time at all!

Sense of humour

Perhaps unexpected, but the bulk of accountancy, be it meeting at a client's office, or preparing financial statements within a trust administration company, will require you to deal with people with grace and good humour – the quickest way to aggravate someone is to be commanding rather than polite!

Intelligence and common sense

The academic qualifications to become an accountant vary widely, depending on the awarding body (see Chapter 3: *Routes into accountancy* for further information), so when intelligence is mentioned, is does not intimate 'above average' or 'genius' levels, but an ability to work with facts and figures (if only to get you through your exams!).

Patience

The need to wait for information to either be provided (such as a set of financial statements) or to become available from a client will require you to be patient and calm rather than impatient.

Politeness and professional courtesy

This extends beyond basic manners to professional courtesy and behaviour, which relates as much to politeness as it does to acting ethically, morally and in the best interests of your employer, client and institute, rather than yourself.

Integrity

A quality set out by many of the awarding bodies (such as AAT and ACCA), integrity refers to being open, honest and ethical in all dealings with clients, the public and others you may be in contact with. An example is **not** using information obtained from your workplace to buy shares in a client with the intention of making a profit (not least because this is illegal, known as insider dealing).

Ambition and drive

Your desire to progress will keep you on track. Whether it is the desire to pass your next exam, to become fully qualified or to be promoted, you will need to maintain focus on your end goals; the ambition and drive to achieve these will help greatly.

Reliability

In some respects this is an extension of time keeping (see the *Skills* section below) and politeness (above). Being reliable is important, regardless of where you work – you will be a key member of a team, department or organisation, so meeting deadlines, doing work to the best of your abilities and being dependable will help not just you but your colleagues.

Skills

Top tip

How to identify and develop your skills

There are certain qualities that you will or will not have, as we can see above. Bear in mind that the qualities are simply a guide; the most important (and simplest) thing is to develop your skills in the following areas:

- Organisation
- Numeracy
- Writing
- Time keeping
- Communication

As with honing any skill, whether it is rehearsing lines for a play, or studying for your final accountancy exams, there is a method: PRACTISE PRACTISE PRACTISE!

Organisation

At first glance, this would appear to be quality rather then a skill – you either are, or are not, an organised person – however, organised people are only this way because they have developed their skills.

Filing documents away upon completion, arranging and co-ordinating meetings between staff members and external parties – these are not innate qualities, but skills that enhance and promote organisation. Try to arrange for a large group of people to attend a gathering, getting them to confirm when they will arrive, how they will get there and when they are leaving. Take on the task of arranging work functions or simply filing your own documents (bank statements, insurance policies, tax forms etc). This is much easier to put into practice in the workplace, where past documents **must** be filed and found at a later date – for example last year's bank statements for the auditors to examine.

Numeracy

Having earlier disputed the belief that accountants are all expert mathematicians, it may appear somewhat contradictory to now tell you that the best way to become one is to work on your numeracy! But the fact is that basic numeracy skills are essential – a calculator will always be to hand (even in your exams) to assist with the trickier calculations.

Assess your skills

Try going online to http://studentvirtuallearn.accaglobal.com to use their self-check modules which will offer a chance of feedback and practice for your numeracy skills.

Writing

The current age of informal, electronic communication – be it a text message or social media post – has led to a considerable lack of formal communication. It may sound a somewhat romantic notion, but in order to develop skills in the appropriate use of grammar, sentence structure and formal communication, try sending emails in the form of a formal letter. Start writing a blog and invite comments regarding your communication style. Formal writing is a skill that will be used both in your written exams and working life, so a useful tool to have.

Assess your skills

Try going online to http://studentvirtuallearn.accaglobal.com to use their self-check modules which will offer a chance of feedback and practice for your English skills.

Time keeping

If you are always late, then buy (and more importantly – **use**) a watch! Practise **p**unctuality **p**ersistently!

When you are training to be an accountant (or even once qualified) it is unacceptable to make your clients wait – they are paying for your time after all. If you work in a regulated environment, deadlines (such as certain document filing deadlines set by the London Stock Exchange) will not wait for you. Start now by turning up on time and your punctual proficiency will be perfect!

Case study:

Amanda runs her own accounting practice. She identifies some of the key skills to be an accountant as follows:

- 'Confidence – you have to make your own decisions and be happy with them.

- Inter-personal skills – clients of small firms generally don't have anyone financial in-house so I'm the one they turn to for straight-forward explanations.

- Time management – as a sole trader with about 130 clients there are a lot of deadlines to keep track of and I have to ensure I do the work in the right order and chase things up at appropriate times to meet them all.

- Technical knowledge – even if I don't know the details of something, I need to know that there is a potential issue so that I can research it or get external advice.'

Communication

Try to speak with clarity, confidence and consistency in whatever you do, whether you are at the pub, or giving a presentation.

Top tip

Four key tips for public speaking are Carry Clubb's four Ps: power, pitch, pace and... pause:

- **Power**: Use the full extent of your voice – project to the back of the room; they want to hear you as much as the people at the front! Breathe deeply from your diaphragm and speak with confidence.

- **Pitch**: Vary the tone of your voice, in order to prevent those listening from losing interest and focus. Change the intonation and emphasis of words in order to highlight a point.

- **Pace**: Do not rush! The most common mistake for people communicating is to rush through, leading to more questions about the topics that were rushed. Speak more slowly and use... (see next point)...

- **Pause**: Combined with pace... a pause... can outline an important point, give people time to digest what you are saying, or act as a juncture to invite questions.

(Reproduced with kind permission of Carry Clubb from Actors in Industry.)

Chapter summary

The qualities required to be an accountant are to be used as a guide only. The chances are, if you are reading this book, you have the desire to become an accountant, and the motivation to understand more about it – these alone will assist you. If you are to succeed as an accountant, your skills are more important, if only for the fact that you can improve these by following our Top tips and practising their use.

Key points

- Consider your qualities in light of the list given in this chapter, but do not worry if you feel you don't have any of them – they are not obligatory!

- Practise your skills in your day-to-day life; they are key if you wish to succeed as an accountant.

Useful resources

ACCA self-check modules: http://studentvirtuallearn.accaglobal.com

Inside Careers, career advice: www.insidecareers.co.uk

Reference

ACCA (2012) *Student VLC*. [Online] Available at: http// studentvirtuallearn.accaglobal.com [Accessed 22 November 2012].

Chapter 3

Routes into accountancy

Clare Buck

Introduction

It has long been believed that accountants are all graduates with maths degrees, business degrees or economics degrees. However, the awarding bodies and indeed, many employers, no longer require trainees to have a degree; some do not demand A levels or Highers, and in certain cases, GCSEs (or equivalent qualifications such as an NVQ / SVQ) are not necessary. With this in mind, let us consider what previous qualifications might be needed to become an accountant.

University

As with almost any career, a degree is considered by many to be the best way for candidates to secure a job – whether they are training to be an actuary, an air traffic controller or an accountant. In general, the *subject* of the degree you choose to undertake is less of an issue than the *class* of degree obtained. For example: a first class honours degree in Natural Science will be more highly regarded by an employer than a 'pass' (or ordinary degree) in Accounting and Finance.

The awarding bodies (ICAS, ICAEW, ACCA, CIMA, AAT, CIPFA etc) do not require you to have a degree, but if you want a degree and believe that accountancy is the way forward, then there are plenty of courses on offer at a wide variety of universities.

Rather than sticking with a single subject, you could choose to diversify and combine accounting with economics, law, marketing, management, Spanish, taxation, computer science or English. The choice of university programmes is wide (as an example, a search for 'accounting' on www.whatuni.com reveals more than 130 degree courses).

The most apparent benefits and drawbacks of obtaining an accountancy degree can be easily summarised – an academic track record versus significant financial outlay.

The specific benefit of having an accountancy degree is that most of the awarding bodies, such as ICAEW, ACCA and CIMA allow graduates (with relevant degrees) to circumvent certain of the professional exams and progress to the latter exams more quickly than candidates who have A levels or unrelated degrees.

The drawbacks of this particular method of entry are prevalent as well, given that, in order to qualify as an accountant, three years' practical experience is required; meaning that graduates will pass their exams more quickly, but remain unable to professionally qualify any more quickly than non-graduates.

Professional accountancy qualifications

There are many different accountancy qualifications, and all have different entry routes and requirements depending on whether you are a school leaver, a graduate or someone working, either within or outside of the sector. It is sometimes difficult to choose the most appropriate qualification, and a question often asked is:

'Which accounting qualification should I study and why?'

The decision depends on a number of factors and there are two important aspects to consider when making it:

1. You need to decide which type of qualification you wish to study for

2. In order to be a full member of the awarding body you need to demonstrate appropriate work experience in a wide range of disciplines

So an important factor in your decision should be the type of employment you currently have, and what career options this will offer you.

Accounting technician or chartered accountancy qualification?

In accountancy there are two different types of qualification you can study for. You can either study the accounting technician route or for a chartered accountancy qualification. It is important to understand that both consist of different levels of study and each is a qualification in its own right. As a potential student you need to appreciate that achieving any of the different examinations and awards adds value to your CV and enhances your employability. The terms 'accounting technician' and 'chartered accountant' refer to the status you will have if you complete the full qualification and demonstrate the right level of work experience to gain full membership of the relevant body.

Accounting Technicians complete qualifications that are recognised on the Qualifications and Credits Framework (QCF) which means that the qualifications are broken down into levels, similar to NVQs, and have a credit value attached to them.

There are currently two accountancy technician qualifications that you can choose from, either the Association of Accounting Technicians (AAT) or the Certified Accounting Technician (CAT) qualification. Both are eligible for funding as part of the UK Government Funded Apprenticeship Scheme and are explained in more detail below.

When it comes to chartered accountancy qualifications there is a lot more choice, and this can often appear rather daunting at first. Again, choosing between them becomes much more simple when you consider the type of work experience you have and can gain while studying, and the type of career in accounting, or otherwise, that you wish to follow. Many employers will have a preferred qualification for their employees so it may be that your employer will direct you as to which to complete.

Each is explained below; all have different membership rules and varying costs for registering as a student, sitting examinations and becoming a full member. You should check each qualification's website for the most up-to-date information before choosing which study route to pursue.

Association of Accounting Technicians (AAT)

The AAT is an awarding body that offers an accounting technician qualification, with three different levels of study from QCF level two to level four. Level two qualifications are roughly similar to GCSEs or equivalent, level three to A levels and level four roughly equates to the first year of an undergraduate degree. Each level of the AAT has a number of different units to complete, from basic accounting at level two through to financial statements, tax and audit at level four.

There are no minimum entry requirements to study the AAT qualification and students can commence their study at any level depending on their work experience and prior knowledge. Very few however start studying at level four and this should not be attempted without significant accounting work experience and advice from the AAT and your training provider.

Most students start their AAT study at either level two or three. Level two includes a solid understanding of the basics of double entry bookkeeping and basic costing techniques so is a good place to start if you don't already have knowledge and work experience relating to these areas.

All three levels of the qualification include papers in financial and management accounting techniques, different levels also cover ethics, spreadsheets and techniques in working effectively. At level four students also have a choice of two from four optional papers, which allows an opportunity to choose papers most relevant to their career – in business tax, personal tax, audit, and credit management.

On completion of your studies you can apply to become a full member of the AAT, and to use the designation MAAT after your name. In order to apply for this you will need to demonstrate an appropriate amount of work experience. On completion of the AAT qualification you can

also claim exemptions from the chartered accountancy qualifications should you wish to continue your studies to one of these. Most offer exemptions from the first level of their qualifications.

The AAT qualification can also lead to higher education opportunities and on completion of the level three qualification students will be accredited with 160 UCAS points. Over 30 universities offer exemptions to AAT professional members for accounting and finance related degrees.

Finally, a MAAT can apply to the AAT to become an AAT licence Member in Practice (MIP), allowing them to run their own accountancy practice.

The AAT qualification takes approximately two to three years to complete depending on the level you commence at, how quickly you study and take the relevant exams, and how often courses are available from your chosen training provider.

Further details on the AAT qualification can be found at www.aat.org.uk.

Foundations in Accountancy (FIA) and Certified Accounting Technician (CAT)

These qualifications are available from the ACCA and are similar in syllabus content to the AAT but have fewer examinations at each level. The CAT qualification is achieved by completing the ACCA's FIA examinations and then specialist option awards – selecting two from three optional papers, which cover tax, financial management and audit.

Although there are fewer examinations on the FIA qualification scheme, FIA is generally less well-known than the AAT in the UK (though FIA has greater overseas prominence) and offers exemptions, on completion, from the ACCA qualification.

The format and content of FIA and CAT are similar to the AAT and overall are made up of four levels of papers, each with a credit value on the QCF. The qualifications cover the same range as the AAT in terms of financial and management accounting and ethics but do not have separate papers available on spreadsheets and working effectively as these skills are embedded in other papers.

Again, similar to the AAT, there are two optional papers to choose from to complete level four; these cover tax, financial management or audit. On completion of the nine exams, students can apply for CAT status by demonstrating at least 12 months' relevant practical experience.

There are no entry requirements for students studying the FIA and CAT qualifications and the ACCA publishes information on how students may claim exemptions from some of the FIA exams on their website.

Students completing the FIA exams can continue onto the professional exams with the aim of achieving ACCA professional status on completion. These professional exams are covered in more detail below.

On average it will take a student between two to three years to complete the CAT qualification, although it can be achieved in less time. One year of relevant practical experience must be demonstrated before achieving CAT status.

Further details on the CAT qualification can be found at: www.accaglobal.com/fia.

Association of Chartered Certified Accountants (ACCA)

The ACCA is a globally recognised accounting qualification and professional body with more than 144,000 members worldwide. It offers both Certified Accounting Technician (CAT) and Chartered Certified Accountant (ACCA) qualifications depending on the exams you wish to undertake.

The entry requirements are that all students without prior qualifications enter at level one – the FIA level – those with technician level or equivalent qualifications (eg CAT) can enter at level two and those who have completed accredited degrees from recognised institutions may enter at level three.

The ACCA qualification consists of three levels of papers, with an award granted after completion of each level. The first level (knowledge level) contains three exams in the basics of accounting. Level two (skills level) offers six papers with a broader scope in topics such as audit, tax, financial reporting and law. Following completion of the second level, students will receive the Advanced Diploma in Accounting and Business and are able to obtain a degree in Applied Accounting from Oxford Brookes University.

The final (professional) stage consists of three compulsory papers and a choice of two from four optional papers, allowing candidates to tailor their finals to their career path. If successful in an application to become a full member, Chartered Certified Accountant status is awarded and recognised in any type of organisation and sector – from accountancy and professional services firms to industry. The ACCA also offers an MBA for members wishing to achieve a generalist business qualification through Oxford Brookes University.

The FIA qualification that forms part of the CAT qualification can also be used as entry to the ACCA qualification if students meet the ACCA's entry requirements to the professional exams.

The full professional qualification consists of 14 exams which, once completed, are combined with at least 36 months' relevant work experience to apply for full membership of the body, allowing members to use the designation ACCA. It takes between three to five years to complete the qualification, depending on exemptions awarded. Further information is available at www.accaglobal.com.

> 'I undertook the ACCA qualification as it suited my learning style. The ACCA exams provided me with the opportunity to control my learning easily, to take up to three exams per sitting and manage my social and work commitments around my training.'

Chartered Institute of Management Accountants (CIMA)

The CIMA offers globally recognised qualifications in management accounting which combine accounting, finance and management. There are over 83,000 members worldwide.

The CIMA qualification consists of four levels, the lowest of which is the CIMA certificate in business accounting; students may be exempt from some or all of this depending on prior qualifications such as AAT or a relevant degree. Those with relevant degrees may also be eligible for exemptions from papers at the higher levels. The CIMA qualification also includes a strategic level, covering strategy management in organisations, culminating in a case study based paper that demonstrates skills in research, analysis and the ability to produce a professional report.

The CIMA qualification is open to anyone, with no formal entry requirements, though as with all accounting qualifications it is recommended that students have a good knowledge and understanding of English and maths.

On completion of the CIMA qualification students can apply to become full members of CIMA by demonstrating three years' relevant, practical experience. CIMA members hold positions in a variety of organisations and sectors and typically work in industry, commerce, management consultancy, banks, and the not-for-profit and private sectors.

CIMA has partnered with certain universities so students can take the opportunity to gain a degree while studying for the CIMA qualification and their website details how this can be achieved. On completion of CIMA members are automatically entitled to become a Chartered Global Management Accountant (CGMA).

The CIMA qualification takes between two to four years to complete depending on exemptions and the pace of study.

More information on the CIMA qualification can be found at www. cimaglobal.com.

Chartered Institute of Public Finance and Accountancy (CIPFA)

The CIPFA is an accounting qualification for those working in public finance, specifically in the public sector, from the NHS to the BBC. It is also relevant to those wishing to work for charities and members also work in the private sector too. There are around 13,500 members worldwide.

There are three stages to the qualification and each consists of a number of modules. On completion of the first and the second, certificate and diploma awards are achieved respectively.

CIPFA's minimum entry requirements are three GCSEs (grade A–C) and two A levels (grade A–C) or equivalent. Students over 21 can take the mature entrance route instead and should have at least three years' relevant work experience and the support of their employer.

Students who have completed the AAT are exempt from certain CIPFA papers. The number depends on the optional papers taken. Those with relevant degrees may be exempt from papers – dependent on the degree taken. Students who have completed ACCA, CIMA ICAS or CAI examinations can apply for CIPFA membership after completing the specific papers in public sector finance.

CIPFA also offers a wide range of certificates and diplomas in specialist areas of public finance. On completion and to qualify for full member status, students must pass the CIPFA examinations and demonstrate around three years' practical work experience (specifically, evidence of at least 400 days' technical exposure must be demonstrated). It also provides practice assurance for members who hold Practising Certificates.

The qualification typically takes three years and on successfully completing all the examinations students are required to demonstrate a log of work-place experience to gain full membership. Upon admission to membership, candidates can use the designatory letters CPFA after their name.

Further details can be found on the CIPFA website: www.cipfa.org.uk.

Institute of Chartered Accountants in England and Wales (ICAEW)

The ICAEW has over 134,000 members in 160 countries and provides an opportunity to study for its ACA qualification. On admission to full membership, members may use the letters ACA after their name.

The ACA qualification consists of three stages of study and each is made up of a number of different modules; stage one (knowledge) consists of six computer-based exams, stage two (application) has six paper-based exams and the final stage is made up of three written papers. The last paper (one of the three finals) is a case study that tests the student's professional skills in the context of a specific business issue.

Entry requirements for the ACA qualification is either for two A levels or a degree. Candidates not meeting the minimum requirements for entry can take the AAT-ACA route instead, being the ICAEW fast track route for students who have completed the AAT qualification. The AAT-ACA fast track is a popular way into the profession but does require trainees to complete a training agreement with one of the ICAEW authorised training employers – full details of this can be found on the ICAEW website.

The ACA qualification also has exemptions for graduates with relevant degrees. The ICAEW has a number of strategic partnerships with universities and employers which allow students to work and / or study for a related degree and the professional qualification. An example is the PwC Flying Start Degree with Newcastle University (see: www.ncl.ac.uk/nubs/undergrad/flyingstart/).

On completion of all 15 ACA exams full membership of the ICAEW can be applied for by demonstrating three years' work experience, completed through a training agreement with an ICAEW approved training organisation. This includes evidencing at least 450 days of technical work experience, evidence of Initial Professional Development and the completion of structured training in ethics.

The ACA qualification typically takes three to four years to complete, and further details can be found at www.icaew.com.

Institute of Chartered Accountants in Scotland (ICAS)

The ICAS is a professional body with around 19,000 members worldwide. ICAS provides the Chartered Accountant (CA) qualification and students must train with an ICAS authorised employer to ensure they gain the relevant practical work experience required for full membership.

There are three levels of study for the CA qualification which test professional competence, skills and expertise; a business ethics module is also required to complete the full qualification.

Students wishing to take the CA qualification can either start as a school leaver or a graduate. School leavers must complete the AAT qualification first and are required to demonstrate at least 12 months' practical work experience. They then need to ensure they have a training contract with an ICAS-approved employer before starting to study for the CA qualification. Graduates also require a training contract. There are also partnerships with universities which allow the study of a degree alongside the CA qualification. An example is the Ernst and Young degree programme with Lancaster University where students study for a BSc (Hons) in Accounting and the CA qualification combined. For more information, refer to: www.lums.lancs.ac.uk.

On completion of the professional qualification and having completed a training contract (usually for three years) demonstrating the relevant work experience requirements and how key competencies have been achieved, students also complete a course and assignment in business ethics before applying for full membership.

Members of the ICAS can apply for practising certificates if applicable and ICAS offers a range of business courses that can be taken to enhance skills and knowledge. Members can use the letters CA after their name; the qualification typically takes between three to five years depending on the entry route.

Further details can be found on the ICAS website: www.icas.org.uk.

The Chartered Accountants of Ireland (CAI)

The CAI (formerly the Institute of Chartered Accountants in Ireland) is the largest and longest established accountancy body in Ireland with more than 20,000 members worldwide.

There are three levels of study consisting of a number of papers at proficiency levels one and two and then a Final Admitting Exam with a core and an elective element.

In 2011 the CAI launched a Chartered Accountants Elevation Programme making the qualification more accessible. Under this programme students can study in the traditional way – under a training contract – but the education and the experience parts of the programme do not need to happen at the same time, so students can commence study without a training contract. Further information as to how this programme works is available on the CAI website.

School leavers can start with the CAI qualification or the Accounting Technicians Ireland qualification (www.accountingtechniciansireland.ie) depending on their prior qualifications. Graduates can commence with the CAI qualification but do require one year's technical work experience before they can sit the final year exams. Graduates may be offered exemptions from some papers depending on relevant prior qualifications, although exemptions are subject to a ten-year time limit.

The amount of work experience required to claim full membership on completion of the qualification depends on the entry route taken but is typically between three to four years in total. Credit can be claimed for relevant work experience prior to starting the qualification up to a maximum of 18 months in total.

The CAI qualification typically takes three to four years to complete and further details can be found at www.charteredaccountants.ie.

Institute:	AAT	CAT	ACCA	CIMA	CIPFA	ICAEW	ICAS	CAI
How many exams?	18	9	14	10	12	15	10	10
How many levels?	3	4	3	4	3	3	3	3
Do I need work experience?	Yes	Yes	Yes	Yes	Yes	Yes	Yes	Yes
How much work experience?	1 year	1 year	3 years	3 years	3 years	3 years	3 years	3–4 years
What letters can I use?	MAAT	CAT	ACCA	ACMA	CPFA	ACA	CA	ACA
What are the minimum entry requirements?	None	None	CAT or 2 A levels	Cert AB*, AAT or degree	AAT or 2 A levels	CFAB#, AAT or 2 A levels	AAT or degree	AAT or 3 A levels

* – CIMA Certificate in Accounting and Business
# – ICAEW Certificate in Accounting and Business

Table 3.1: Summary of qualifications

Funding for training

There are different options for funding your study for accounting qualifications depending on the route you choose to take and the type of employment contract you enter into. Students can have their training fully or partially funded, either as part of an apprenticeship, funded by the Skills Funding Agency (SFA), or by their employer. Students may also pay for their training themselves and if this is the case they may be eligible for a Professional and Career Development Loan to assist with paying for the training until the qualification is complete. More details on these can be found at: www.gov.uk.

The various options are discussed below and it should be remembered that each qualification and awarding body has different student registration, exam and membership fees and the choice of training provider will also impact on the total cost of completing your studies.

Skills Funding Agency apprenticeship funding

The Financial Skills Partnership (FSP) accredits official apprenticeship frameworks in accounting that are funded by the SFA for all students eligible for apprenticeship funding. To be eligible, students must be non-graduates, and have the right to live and work in the UK, and be in accountancy-related employment. Full and up-to-date eligibility criteria can be checked with the National Apprenticeship Service (NAS) at www.apprenticeships.org.uk.

It should be noted that an apprenticeship can be completed by any student but cannot be funded by the SFA unless the student is eligible under the criteria current at the time of application for an apprenticeship place.

An apprenticeship framework consists of a competence and a knowledge qualification and, in the case of the current accountancy framework, these are combined into one relevant qualification with students on an apprenticeship completing one level of either the AAT or the FIA qualification as outlined earlier. Each level of these qualifications is an apprenticeship in its own right so students can be funded for all three levels if required, if they can demonstrate that the level they are working at has progressed in line with the advancement of their studies.

Such frameworks do not just consist of the career relevant qualifications (in this case, accounting) but also include two other requirements – the completion of an Employment Rights and Responsibilities (ERR) workbook, and the completion of Key or Functional Skills in English and Mathematics. Students may be exempt from these if they hold GCSEs or equivalent qualifications and apprenticeship providers will be able to advise as to whether they need to be completed or not.

Only on the completion of all the framework requirements, and not just the accounting qualification, is an apprenticeship deemed to be complete so students embarking on this path should be aware of the additional requirements, although it should be noted that these should be relatively straightforward to complete.

For eligible students aged 16–18 an apprenticeship is fully funded by the UK government so this is an excellent opportunity for school leavers to commence their accountancy career – although as previously mentioned an apprentice does need to be in relevant employment as part of the eligibility criteria. Many organisations are beginning to recruit school leavers into the profession and there are many apprenticeship opportunities open to young people. Many of the large accountancy firms now have school leaver intakes at least equivalent to their graduate intake and many smaller firms only recruit at this level. It is more usual for such recruitment to be at 18, post A level, but there are some opportunities for younger students. Similar opportunities exist within other accountancy career paths such as industry and the public sector.

Many organisations use the Apprenticeship Vacancy Matching Service (AVMS) to advertise such vacancies and this can be accessed at https://apprenticeshipvacancymatchingservice.lsc.gov.uk. Organisations also advertise their apprenticeship vacancies on their own websites and with third party organisations such as notgoingtouni (www.notgoingtouni.co.uk).

Students aged 19 plus should have part of the cost of their training funded by their employer and apprenticeship training providers ask for different employer contributions based on their individual requirements.

Other types of apprenticeship

Some organisations offer their own apprenticeship schemes, not funded by the UK government but by the employer themselves. Depending on the employer these will offer training in either the accounting technician or chartered qualifications and sometimes for school leavers will include both. Some employers prefer students to start with the accounting technician qualifications and progress onto chartered accountancy qualifications upon completion. With such schemes, the employer often also ensures that the trainee gains experience in different parts of the organisation to widen their skills and knowledge.

Top tip

Many organisations will utilise apprenticeship funding for eligible employees while they study for the accounting technician qualifications so vacancies may be advertised as outlined in the section on apprenticeships. Employers will use careers fairs and similar opportunities to advertise their schemes and attract talent, plus they usually have a dedicated section of their organisation's website for recruitment so it is a good investment to spend a little time reviewing websites if there are certain organisations you wish to consider working for.

Other work-based funding

As accounting may be required for staff to do their jobs, many employers will help their staff towards the cost of funding training in accountancy qualifications. Each employer will have different schemes and support the trainee in different ways – both in terms of support towards the payment of fees and time off for training – so it is worth speaking to your employer, or asking potential employers, about their policies before starting to study. Many employers support their staff in this way as it is important that an accountant knows their employer's systems, processes and culture in order to operate effectively and it can sometimes be more cost-effective to train and support existing staff than to recruit externally.

See Chapter 6 for more information on where to find work.

Self-funding your accountancy training

Funding your own accountancy training is a huge investment in your career. Although it can be very expensive it can also compare favourably with the cost of going to university and so is an important aspect to consider when deciding your route to becoming an accounting technician or chartered accountant.

Different qualifications have different fees for registration, examinations and membership and although this may have some influence on your decision as to which qualification to study for, it is more important to approach self-funding your training as an investment that you should benefit from on completion, rather than considering the shorter term impact. You should pick the qualification that best suits your career aspirations rather than based on the cost of completion.

If you are self-funding your training the cheapest route may be to self study, from text books, but it should be remembered that this is a difficult (and lonely!) path to undertake and that success rates in examinations are significantly lower for students studying in this way. It therefore may not be the most effective option, as you will end up paying for exam resits and updated text books.

A more expensive option, but one that usually results with a higher rate of passing the examinations, is to invest in training courses and there are many providers to choose from – both in the public and the private sector, (see www.bpp.com for options from one of the UK's leading professional education providers).

There are a range of different study options for classroom training including day release, evening and weekend classes plus specific taught and revision courses. Different providers offer different packages and many release their examination pass rates so it is worth spending some time researching the alternative choices before deciding on this type of investment.

Chapter summary

This chapter has explained that there is no requirement to have a degree in order to train as an accountant. Anyone, regardless of their (academic or employment) background, can choose to train as an accountant. The variety of institutes and qualifications allows greater flexibility in terms of time and learning style, so weigh each one up carefully. Although professional qualifications are costly, there are sponsorship and apprentice options available.

Key points

- The first decision you might need to make is: do you want or need a degree?

- The second is: would you like to be an accounting technician or chartered accountant?

- Each institute has their own benefits, so the choice is yours!

- Your future progression will only ever be helped by having a professional qualification.

- Finally, it is often better for you to work alongside an employer (whether as an apprentice or graduate trainee), as you will get relevant work experience, while they will pay for your exams (it is very costly to self-fund).

Useful resources

What Uni: www.whatuni.com

AAT: www.aat.org.uk

FIA: www.accaglobal.com/fia

ACCA: www.accaglobal.com

CIMA: www.cimaglobal.com

CIPFA: www.cipfa.org.uk

ICAEW: www.icaew.com

ICAS: www.icas.org.uk

CAI: www.charteredaccountants.ie

Accounting Technicians Ireland: www.accountingtechniciansireland.ie

Professional and Career Development Loan: www.direct.gov.uk

Apprenticeships: www.apprenticeships.org.uk

Apprenticeships Vacancy Matching Service:
https://apprenticeshipvacancymatchingservice.lsc.gov.uk

Notgoingtouni: www.notgoingtouni.co.uk

BPP Professional Education: www.bpp.com

References

AAT (2012), *What We Do*. [Online] Available at: www.aat.org.uk/about-aat/what-we-do [Accessed 22 November 2012].

ACCA (2012), *About Us*. [Online] Available at: www.accaglobal.com/en/discover/about.html [Accessed 22 November 2012].

Accounting Technicians Ireland (2012) *About Us*. [Online] Available at: www.accountingtechniciansireland.ie/About_Us/ [Accessed 22 November 2012].

Apprenticeships (2012) *Access to Apprenticeships*. [Online] Available at: www.apprenticeships.org.uk/Partners/Policy/AccesstoApprenticeships.aspx [Accessed 22 November 2012].

Apprenticeships (2012) *Accounting – Apprenticeships*. [Online] Available at: www.apprenticeships.org.uk/Types-of-Apprenticeships/Business-Administration-and-Law/Accounting.aspx [Accessed 22 November 2012].

CAI (2012) *Chartered Accountants Ireland Global*. [Online] Available at: www.charteredaccountants.ie/General/About-Us/Chartered-Accountants-Ireland-Global [Accessed 22 November 2012].

CIMA (2012) *About Us*. [Online] Available at: www.cimaglobal.com/About-us/ [Accessed 22 November 2012].

CIPFA (2012) *About CIPFA*. [Online] Available at: www.cipfa.org/About-CIPFA [Accessed 22 November 2012].

GOV.UK (2012) *Professional and Career Development Loan*. [Online] Available at: www.gov.uk/career-development-loans [Accessed 22 November 2012].

Financial Reporting Council, Public Oversight Body (2011) *Key Facts & Trends Reports, 2011*. [Online] Available at: www.frc.org.uk/getattachment/1b7baf93-3be3-4fba-b4c1-dec90874b23d/Key-Facts-and-Trends-in-the-Accountancy-Profession-27-June-2011.aspx [Accessed 22 November 2012].

ICAEW (2012) *Who We Are, About Us*. [Online] Available at: www.icaew.com/en/about-icaew/who-we-are [Accessed 22 November 2012].

ICAS (2012) *What We Do*. [Online] Available at: http://icas.org.uk/What_we_do.aspx [Accessed 22 November 2012].

What Uni? (2012) *Accounting Degree Courses*. [Online] Available at: www.whatuni.com [Accessed 22 November 2012].

Chapter 4

Roles and specialisations in accountancy

Lucy Freckleton

Introduction

In this chapter we are going to look at some of the different job roles and specialisations in accountancy. Evidently, we can only provide a taster of these in this book, so if any interest you we would encourage you to do some more research.

Top tip

The internet has a whole host of useful resources, but why not try to find someone working in a specific role and find out what they do and what they enjoy? Applying for work experience is an excellent way of obtaining a better idea of what is involved.

A career in accountancy gives you great choice and flexibility. If you ask accountants about their careers, you'll find that many have worked in a number of different roles and enjoyed a wide variety of experiences. Becoming an accountant opens doors for you and provides opportunities that few other careers offer.

Public practice or professional services

In public practice, accountancy firms offer services to clients. This could be a Big Four firm offering a range of products (such as audit and tax structuring) to international companies through to individual accountants preparing accounts and tax returns for small businesses.

Audit

Auditors provide a vital service to investors. They report to the shareholders of a business on whether 'in their opinion' the financial statements of a company show a 'true and fair view' of the company's financial performance (what they have earned and spent) and position (how much it is worth) and to ensure that the accounts comply with relevant laws and regulations.

Many accountants start their careers in audit. Typically, graduates are awarded a training contract (see Chapter 6) with a firm in public practice and work as part of an audit team servicing clients within a broad range of industry sectors. If you want to progress in this area you will need post qualification experience to become a qualified auditor.

What does an audit involve?

As part of an audit team you would visit the client's premises and examine various documents and obtain evidence in order to confirm that the value of the client's assets and liabilities stated on their balance sheet agrees to your estimation. This might involve investigating, for example, whether debts owed by customers are likely to be repaid in full or whether goods held in the warehouse are worth the value stated in the accounts. You might be involved in reviewing the income statement and checking that it represents a true and fair view of the financial performance of the client and asking: does the income all relate to the period being reviewed? Have all the expenses for the year been included?

An audit would also involve reviewing the financial controls a client has in place and considering whether they are adequate in light of the risks facing that business.

Definition

Controls

Often referred to as **internal controls**, this is the collection of procedures, checks and reviews in place to help control and monitor a company's transactions.

Controls exist for many reasons, such as to prevent or detect fraud or non-compliance with laws. For example controls over cash in a restaurant would be to lock it in a safe, bank it regularly and use CCTV to observe those handling the cash, thus preventing theft.

Career progression

Many accountants train in audit departments, then move into other areas after qualification. Audit gives a great foundation in understanding how a business operates and develops skills that are useful in many other areas, such as analysis and review. Some people move into industry (such as working for a bank or manufacturing company), while others may stay in public practice and specialise in tax or corporate finance.

For those who want to remain in audit there is the possibility of developing industry specialisms, promotion to partner and a chance to get involved in the management of the firm and in winning new client work.

What skills do you need?

You need to have good analytical skills so that you can make sense of large amounts of financial data to identify trends and areas requiring further investigation. You also need the ability to assess the risks facing a particular company, which will help identify key priorities for audit work.

Audit work is done in teams, so your ability to work well with others and manage and develop junior staff will be important as your career progresses. When you first start work in an audit team you may be asked to do some administrative tasks that all trainees will be expected to undertake. They may appear uninteresting but it is important that you get on with them to support your colleagues.

Good communication skills are essential. You will have to get information from junior client staff as well as directors. Some client staff will be apprehensive about talking to members of the audit team (often feeling that they are personally under scrutiny) so your ability to build relationships quickly and relate to a wide variety of people is essential. You will also be involved in writing reports summarising your findings and offering advice to your audit clients so your written communication skills need to be strong.

You need to have a strong sense of ethics. Auditors have been targeted in recent years, sometimes unfairly, for their inability to detect significant fraud for example at Enron, or their failure to prevent the financial crisis of 2008 and the collapse of financial institutions such as Lehman Brothers. It is likely that the role of auditor will continue to change as investors demand greater reassurance from audit work.

The best bits

Ask auditors what they enjoy and invariably they'll say the variety of working with different clients, the exposure to a range of industries, the camaraderie of working in smaller teams and the great training they receive.

Within a matter of months, your role in audit will give you an understanding of a wide variety of industries, entities and systems that few other entry-level accountancy roles can match.

Case study: An auditor's perspective

Steve worked for a small accountancy practice after graduation. Following a good grounding in accounting work, he joined a Big Four audit department. Steve was attracted to public practice because of the quality of training and support given; he also liked the idea of working and training with a peer group.

Steve says:

'Every client is different, has different systems, business strategies and people. Internally you get to work with a different team on each job – there can't be that many careers where you have that variety.'

Steve also enjoyed the discrete nature of each assignment:

'There is always a clear conclusion with a clearance meeting or report to the client and ultimately a set of financial statements with an opinion which allows a certain amount of job satisfaction when you complete an assignment.'

The challenges

*   You will have to manage tight reporting deadlines and also deal with a number of different clients who will be demanding your attention at the same time.

*   Keeping up to date with changes in accounting standards and other legislation means continued professional development is required.

*   Anyone choosing audit as a career must have the ability to challenge information, ask difficult questions and keep investigating items even when the client is being unsympathetic!

Taxation

Most companies and individuals have to pay some kind of tax. Tax legislation is vast and complex, so wealthy individuals and organisations need help to calculate their tax bill (tax compliance) and take advantage of the myriad of tax breaks and allowances in order to reduce the amount of tax payable in the future (tax planning).

Working in a tax department is more office based than an audit role, but still requires a high degree of client contact. You'll need to obtain information from your client in order to produce their tax returns as well as explaining to them the different options they have in planning their tax affairs.

You'll be involved in representing your clients to the tax authorities, so being able to argue your client's case well is essential to a successful career.

There are several routes to take to qualify as a tax advisor, which can be done after, or instead of, becoming an accountant. Have a look at Chapter 5 for further details.

Career progression

If you know that you want to work in tax, you might look to join a tax department straight away. Other accountants move to tax after they have qualified as an accountant to gain broader commercial experience. There are also opportunities post qualification to work for companies in industry who have internal tax departments.

Case study: The tax advisor cometh...

Naomi decided on an accountancy career after completing her A levels. Rather than studying for a degree she completed her AAT qualification, then went on to qualify as a chartered accountant.

She started her training in an audit department in a medium-sized firm after which she went to work in general practice for a small accounting firm providing accounting and tax services to a range of clients, including several charities.

At this stage, she decided to specialise in taxation and went on to complete her CTA exams. She is now a director of a Top 25 accounting firm and is responsible for corporate tax planning services where she provides advice to owner-managed businesses.

Naomi gets great satisfaction from seeing the tangible results of her work:

'It's great to see businesses paying less tax because of our advice or being able to attract new investors because we've helped them qualify for the Enterprise Investment Scheme.'

One of her career highlights was being able to get agreement from the tax authorities on the tax status of one of her clients:

'It took two years but I won the argument, which was worth £1.8m in tax to my client.'

What skills do you need?

Attention to detail is required as well as the ability to interpret and keep abreast of the constantly developing tax legislation. A good knowledge of the business and the industry your client operates in is important – you need to understand the business and how it makes money before you are able to facilitate any tax advantages.

Problem-solving skills are key as you will need to find innovative ways of reducing your client's tax bill while remaining within the limits of legislation. This can become very complex when you start considering how to do this for an international corporation and need to consider tax regulations in other countries too!

Communication skills are important, as you will need to be able to explain complex tax matters to clients with limited tax knowledge. It is also important to be self-motivated and be an effective independent worker, as you will be responsible for individual clients' tax affairs.

The best bits

This is a good career for those of you that enjoy an intellectual challenge! It's very satisfying to be able to provide advice to clients in this tricky area and become a trusted advisor.

The challenges

Managing competing client needs is a challenge, especially when everyone has the same deadlines and clients only provide you with information at the last minute...

Corporate finance

Corporate finance relates to anything that deals with how businesses fund their activities. Common activities in a corporate finance department are providing services to businesses looking to raise finance through the issue of new shares and giving advice on investments such as the acquisition of another company.

If you work in corporate finance, you might get involved in due diligence, where you review the financial information for a potential acquisition of a smaller company to help determine the value of the business and ensure that there will be no unexpected consequences following completion of the purchase. Some of this work can be carried out in the office but may also require you to visit the target company to review documents and talk to the staff.

> **Definition**
>
> **Due diligence**
>
> **Due diligence** involves investigating the background of a company prior to its purchase (known as the 'target'). This may include whether any bank loans or other debts are held by the target, whether there are any legal proceedings underway against or involving the target or whether the target has complied with all necessary laws and regulations (such as emissions laws for a manufacturing company).

You may also prepare reports required to help raise new finance (such as a loan from a bank) and give advice on how best to do this. This would require a detailed analysis of a company's financial performance.

Career progression

Many accountants who work in corporate finance start off in audit and specialise in corporate finance after qualification. However, there are opportunities for graduates, often those with relevant degrees, to start their training in a corporate finance department.

As well as opportunities in public practice, large companies can have their own in-house corporate finance department. There are opportunities in these departments for school leavers or graduates as well as for recently qualified accountants.

What skills do you need?

You need to be able to quickly comprehend a large amount of financial information in a short period of time. You must have excellent analytical skills and you will spend time building and using financial models to assist with this.

You need to have good communication skills. You will be liaising with lawyers and other professional advisors involved in the transaction, as well as dealing with staff at the company to be purchased who are concerned about the acquisition. Work needs to be done with a high degree of confidentiality.

You need to be able to think quickly and creatively, and have the confidence to ask searching questions. Teamwork is important; corporate finance assignments can require long hours to meet deadlines. Being able to support other team members as well as delivering your own tasks during a deal will ensure success.

The best bits

Corporate finance is an exciting area where the work is fast paced. It is great for those who enjoy doing something new all the time.

Case study: Corporate finance – acquire some variety!

After graduating with a degree in biological sciences, Sue went to work for a Big Four firm in their audit department. After qualifying she became involved in several corporate finance engagements for her audit clients which included advising on rights issues and new placings of shares to fund acquisitions. She then went to work for a UK plc where she was involved in the acquisition and disposal of companies in the UK, Europe and US.

Sue enjoys the variety of the work, carrying out assignments both in the UK and overseas. She gets great satisfaction from seeing that her effort makes a significant contribution. One of her highlights was uncovering that most of the sales of a potential target company were falsified. Finding this early on saved the company time and money and helped avoid a disastrous investment.

The challenges

When you are working on a particular transaction, you can expect to work long hours to meet demanding deadlines. Clients are relying on you to provide advice on areas that have a significant impact on their business. The stakes are high if you fail to identify problems with a client's investment.

Corporate recovery and insolvency

Corporate recovery is the business of assisting ailing companies to restructure their finances to provide stability for the future. If it is not possible to salvage a business then the job of the insolvency practitioner is to close it down in a way that will get the best deal for the parties who are owed money by the company (known as creditors). With high profile companies in difficulty in the news on a regular basis, insolvency practitioners are busy people!

The work is varied and will involve working at the company's premises to obtain financial information for the creditors of the business, organise meetings with the creditors and communicate on a day-to-day basis with staff. Making staff redundant or some involvement in trying to sell parts or the whole of a business may also be part of the role.

Career progression

Although you can now study directly for an insolvency qualification it is common for people to gain an accountancy qualification first. See Chapter 5 for further information on insolvency qualifications. There are limited opportunities for school leavers or graduates to join a corporate recovery and insolvency department but many more once you are a qualified accountant.

What skills do you need?

You need good analytical skills to identify the financial position of a company. You also need great communication skills as you will be dealing with many different people including staff concerned about their jobs and creditors worried about losing their money.

The best bits

You can guarantee work during a recession!

There is a great sense of satisfaction if a company is able to find financial stability again. Every assignment is different and you will get to know a business and its industry incredibly well.

Case study: Corporate recovery – an interesting choice

Sarah graduated with a degree in accounting and financial management. She joined the corporate recovery department of a Big Four firm as it seemed more exciting than audit. She was involved in the running of businesses that had got into financial difficulty, verifying the value of inventory, collecting money from parties who owed money to the company, organising creditor and staff meetings. As well as enjoying the variety of work she relished working in a team that had such a vital role.

The challenges

The insolvency exams are some of the toughest to pass. Corporate recovery teams have to respond quickly to new clients so it is harder to plan your life around work, and you may also find that you are working long hours and travelling away from home regularly.

You are going to have to take tough decisions about the future of a company and people's jobs. You will need to be calm in order to do the job in a fair way and to deal with people at a time of crisis.

Forensic accountancy

If you fancy yourself as a bit of a Sherlock Holmes then maybe you should consider a career in forensic accountancy! Forensic accountancy is a relatively new area of expertise and has gained more exposure in the last 20 years with high profile corporate fraud cases such as Enron, Madoff and Barings Bank – to name a few.

One of the first forensic accountants, Frank J Wilson, led a successful investigation to convict Al 'Scarface' Capone of tax evasion in 1931. Forensic accountants are needed to investigate economic crime such as fraud and money laundering; they also trace misappropriated funds and assets, trying to ensure they are reclaimed. Forensic accountants will be involved in investigating corporate fraud, seizing information and conducting interviews.

Forensic accountants also act as expert witnesses in court cases where there are disputes between companies; they also quantify losses from insurance claims. There are some inventive uses of forensic accountancy – in 2008, Heather Mills recruited a team of forensic accountants to produce an independent valuation of the assets of Paul McCartney in the hope of gaining a greater divorce settlement!

Career progression

There are a few graduate opportunities with specialist forensic accountancy firms but more commonly people move into this area post qualification. All Big Four firms have forensic accountancy departments and many large firms also provide this service.

What skills do you need?

Many of the skills are similar to those required in audit. You need to have an excellent eye for detail and up-to-date technical knowledge to spot irregular accounting entries. You may need to search through files of detailed accounting information before coming across anything significant.

Just like Sherlock, you will need to be able to piece together information to deduce what has happened so the mental agility to solve complex problems is essential.

Extracting information from IT systems is vital to the forensic accountant. IT specialists usually do this, but it is useful for the forensic accountant to be computer literate.

The best bits

Getting to the bottom of a fraud case or securing the best outcome for your client is very satisfying.

The challenges

You will often be working to tight deadlines in a difficult environment and some investigations can take a very long time to complete. Investigations into the US company Enron were still being conducted six years after fraud was initially discovered.

General practice

Some accountants don't necessarily want to choose a specialism and prefer to provide a range of services to small companies. Smaller accountancy firms or individual accountants (known as sole practitioners) working on their own will provide these general practice services.

Case study: General practice – a broad remit

After studying economics at university Amanda went to work for a small accountancy practice. She enjoyed the variety of client work as well as gaining experience of the different industries they operated in. Amanda began her career in the audit and accounts department but later became involved with personal tax and providing accounting services to charities and trusts.

After moving to a larger firm and a promotion to manager Amanda decided to set up her own practice:

'I had got to the stage where I had actually stopped doing the work I enjoyed and was just managing people, problems and deadlines. I was also less directly involved with clients and missed that.'

Amanda now provides accounting and tax services to over 130 clients. She says:

'I enjoy seeing a whole job through from start to finish rather than just reviewing it. I get great satisfaction from allaying clients' fears over their taxes and in discussing their businesses with them in the light of their financial results.'

There are challenges though, and working for yourself means that you must personally manage difficult clients, company cash flow and everything else in between.

Private practice, industry or internal providers

Working as an accountant for one company (rather than providing services to several clients) means you can really get involved with a business and contribute to its success. Every company is different, so it is difficult to give a generic overview of what a role in industry is like. In smaller companies you would perform a range of tasks and cover aspects of management accounting, financial accounting and treasury whereas in large international corporations you would focus more on analysing results for one particular product (such as smartphones or sports cars) or geographical area (such as Europe or North America).

Jobs will vary according to the industry the company operates in. Manufacturing companies need accountants to provide accurate and up-to-date information about product costs; whereas charities need information to assess how effective their fundraising activities are (ie how much money they are spending compared to how much they have coming in).

Career progression is varied – there are opportunities to work as an accountant in industry as either a school leaver or graduate. Further opportunities open up for those wanting to move to industry after qualification in public practice. You could progress to financial director or CEO of a company!

Management accountant

The role of a management accountant varies significantly between industries and companies. Essentially it is concerned with providing internal financial information so the business can be effectively managed; for example gathering the precise costs of making a product compared to its selling price and ensuring that the sales price is higher.

As a management accountant you can expect to be involved in preparing monthly reports showing the financial performance and position of the company, providing explanations as to why the company is doing better or worse than expected (usually by comparing to the financial plan, called the budget). You might get involved in preparing budgets or supporting non-financial managers (eg the production team) by providing them with information to support their decision-making or challenging them on their spending.

Case study: Management accounting – internal route to success

Matt graduated with a degree in civil engineering and joined a large engineering company on a financial management scheme. He qualified as an accountant with CIMA and chose this route as he was keen to be exposed to more commercial decision-making than he felt he would have gained in public practice. He went on to join an international company where he had a variety of roles both in Holland and in the UK. He is currently the UK finance director of another international company. He has a wide-ranging role that includes responsibility for IT and human resources as well as being responsible for most of the merger and acquisition activity in the UK.

Matt says:

'You need to be able to see what is important in the business and provoke discussion about keeping focus on what will really make a difference to the company.'

Career progression

Many companies will employ management accountants either on their own, or as part of a larger team. There are opportunities for school leavers or graduates. It is worth noting here that if you choose to qualify with CIMA, it does not limit you to only being a management accountant – see Chapter 5 for further information on the qualifications available.

What skills do you need?

You are going to be working in a finance team; you therefore need to develop valuable working relationships to obtain the information you need in order to provide the best information for the business. Most management accounting roles will include supporting other parts of the business and explaining financial issues to non-financial managers. The ability to explain and break down financial results and terminology in written reports and verbally is important.

In order to produce financial information, data needs to be collected in a system then used to produce reports. You may get involved in detailed analysis, which will require you to summarise large amounts of data using spreadsheets. Computer literacy and a willingness to learn IT skills will help you get ahead.

Being a management accountant is not just about manipulating numbers and producing reports. As you progress in your career, you will get involved in decision-making – the ultimate direction of the business

– and it is important that you can understand what the numbers are telling you about the business and that you are able to challenge management.

The best bits

As you progress in a company it can be very satisfying to contribute to decision-making and see the business develop.

Working in a team is another hugely enjoyable aspect of the role; it is fun supporting other non-finance areas within the business who really appreciate your financial skills.

The challenges

Producing financial reports at month end and year end can require you to work longer hours. Some people find preparing the same reports and information on a regular basis becomes repetitive.

Financial accountant

The role of a financial accountant covers the production of financial statements for shareholders and potential investors. In a large organisation this may include consolidating the results of a number of different divisions and subsidiaries to produce group accounts. You might also get involved in investor relations and presenting results at board meetings.

Case study: Financial accounting – more than just financial statements

Philippa left school after GCSEs but after enjoying work experience in an accounts office, she took an A level in Accounting and then started her ACCA accountancy studies.

She has worked in treasury departments of large multinational companies, for a software company as an assistant financial controller, and is currently working for a financing business. In this role she has been responsible for preparing statutory accounts and liaising with the external auditors for the annual audit.

For those that enjoy problem-solving, getting the accounts ready for reporting is a satisfying task. Philippa has chosen to work on a contracting basis and she is often engaged by a company to complete reconciliations that haven't been kept up to date or properly maintained. She says that her work is like 'getting paid to do puzzles'. She also enjoys finding ways to improve processes to make reporting more effective.

Career progression

Most companies in industry will employ a financial accountant, or team of financial accountants to prepare the statutory (annual) financial statements and to report to key stakeholders (shareholders, management, the bank or relevant regulators). There are opportunities for school leavers or graduates in a variety of different industries.

What skills do you need?

You need attention to detail to ensure that accounting entries have been correctly entered in the company's financial records. You also need the ability to solve problems when preparing accounts. Accounting systems can be complex so a degree of computer literacy and willingness to work with IT is beneficial.

Communication skills are important as you liaise with shareholders as well as the external auditors, lawyers, tax advisors, bankers and other company advisors.

The best bits

Producing financial accounts lets you see the whole picture of the company you are working for; working to – and meeting – a strict deadline is satisfying, as is communicating with internal and external parties.

The financial statements have to comply with a number of external laws and regulations, allowing you to develop your legal understanding as well as your accounting knowledge.

The challenges

There may be pressure for you to show results that don't accurately reflect the financial performance and position of the company, so a strong sense of ethics and integrity is required.

The finance environment is constantly changing and, with applicable legislation and accounting standards being frequently updated, you need to keep abreast of areas that may have an impact on the business you work for.

Internal audit

Internal audit involves assessing risks faced by a business and ensuring that appropriate controls are in place to mitigate them. You may need to visit different branches and divisions of the business to check that internal procedures are being followed, and then report your findings to senior management. You will also need to be able to provide solutions where problems are identified and work with teams in other areas of the business to implement the solutions. The work could include overseas travel if you work for an international organisation.

Internal audit roles have become increasingly important in recent years, as organisations have had to strengthen corporate governance and controls in response to high profile frauds and business failures.

Much of the work that internal auditors do is similar to that carried out by an external auditor and many of the same skills are required. The scope of the work is much broader and will include reviewing strategic and operational risks as well as financial ones.

> **Definition**
>
> **Internal versus external auditors**
>
> **External auditors** are independent practitioners of the company who provide an opinion on the truth and fairness of the financial statements. They report to the shareholders.
>
> **Internal auditors** are employees of the company who inspect internal information (whether in response to fraud or breach of the law) in great detail – their work is decided by management to whom they also report.

Career progression

Due to the nature of the work, and size of internal audit teams, opportunities usually exist for qualified accountants, however, there may be opportunities available for graduates and school leavers. It is usual for those in internal audit to become a qualified accountant, although there are specific internal audit qualifications available, such as those offered by the Chartered Institute of Internal Auditors.

What skills do you need?

You will need good communication skills, as you will be working with a wide range of staff across the organisation. Not only do you need to be able to engage with people on many different levels, you must also be able to prepare and present reports to senior management.

The internal audit function is only effective if it is strong enough to challenge senior management, so an ability to ask probing questions and strength of character to stand your ground on important matters is essential.

Some of the work will be focused on specific areas of the business but a good internal auditor will always consider the 'big picture,' ie how these different elements of the business impact on the *overall performance* of the company.

The best bits

An internal audit role is a great way to get to know a business. You will gain a good understanding of the whole company and how the different business areas fit together.

You will get exposure to senior management early on, which is interesting and useful for further career progression.

Internal audit gives you a good view of the different roles accountants have within a business so you can assess what other roles you might like to undertake later on in your career.

The challenges

Internal audit teams tend to be small and you need to be able to work on your own and be self-motivated.

Although you are an employee of the company you are still an auditor and will need to try to retain a level of independence from the rest of the business areas. This could be frustrating for someone who wants to get involved in commercial decision-making.

Treasury function

The treasury function covers the following key elements within an organisation:

- Raising finance for the business, for example through bank loans or an issue of shares

- Forecasting future cash requirements

- Managing financial risks such as returns on investments and exposure to variable foreign exchange rates and interest rates (eg the amount paid by the company on a loan).

Overall the treasury function must ensure that a company's finances are managed to achieve the business's desired goals, such as expanding overseas or selling more products.

All businesses require a treasury function. In a small company, the management accountant may also undertake a treasury role. In a large organisation a dedicated team will provide these services.

Career progression

If you have a relevant degree it is possible to secure a treasury position and study for a qualification in treasury rather than qualifying as an accountant first. See Chapter 5 for further details.

What skills do you need?

You need to be good at building relationships, especially with banks, other finance providers and external advisors as well as key personnel within your own organisation.

Treasurers have to make very important decisions, taking responsibility for deals covering significant sums of money, so, you'll need confidence and resolve to do your job.

As you may be dealing with large amounts of money it is important that you have good attention to detail and can remain focussed on a task to avoid costly mistakes! It is also important that you are happy working in an environment with many different policies and procedures – these are vital to ensure that the company's money is properly safeguarded.

You need to be able to analyse information and understand the implications for the company in the event of changes in the economic environment.

The best bits

Treasurers have a wide variety of work and operate at the very heart of a business. In a large corporation they will get a great perspective of the overall business, and many accountants choose this role as a way to get involved in high level business strategy.

Although treasury departments are busy places where the work is demanding, hours of work tend to be more regular than for other advisory roles as deals are usually made during bank trading hours.

The challenges

The sums involved in deals made in large treasury departments can be staggering! The responsibility of looking after the money can prove challenging, but with regular hours, could be a good choice for those who seek consistency and structure in a role.

Chapter summary

The bulk of accountants train with facts and figures, but that does not limit your options to the preparation of financial statements or the auditing of financial information, there are many options open to you in terms of the work and the organisation. Try to find an area of work that interests you – whether it is tax or treasury – as this will make it easier to put in the required work and commitment to gain your qualification.

Key points

- Decide whether you would prefer to go into public practice or private practice and industry.
- Roles are hugely varied and you can tailor your job to your skill set.
- Any qualification you decide to do will be of use, see Chapter 5 for more information.

Useful resources

Association of Corporate Treasurers: www.treasurers.org

Chartered Institute of Internal Auditors: www.iia.org.uk

Inside Careers: www.insidecareers.co.uk

Insolvency exams advice: www.insolvencyexams.co.uk

Network of Independent Forensic Accountants: www.nifa.co.uk

References

Association of Corporate Treasurers (2012) *The Role of a Treasurer.* [Online] Available at: www.treasurers.org/careers/whatistreasury [Accessed 22 November 2012].

Careerplayer (2012) *Accounting and Financial Services.* [Online] Available at: www.careerplayer.com/graduate-jobs/accounting-and-financial-services.aspx [Accessed 22 November 2012].

Chartered Institute of Internal Auditors (2012) *What is Internal Audit?* [Online] Available at: www.iia.org.uk/en/about_us/What_is_internal_audit/index.cfm [Accessed 22 November 2012].

HowStuffWorks (2011) *How Forensic Accounting Works.* [Online] Available at: http://science.howstuffworks.com/forensic-accounting2.htm [Accessed 22 November 2012].

Network of Independent Forensic Accountants (2012) *What is Forensic Accounting?* [Online] Available at: www.nifa.co.uk/forensic-accounting.cfm [Accessed 22 November 2012].

Chapter 5

Further training

Sadie Farrington

Introduction

For some individuals the idea of further study is unthinkable after the marathon of accountancy examinations required in order to qualify. However, it is an undeniable fact that many qualified accountants quickly look for opportunities for new academic challenges as soon as the ordeal of their accountancy finals has subsided! In this chapter we shall look at some of the most common specialist qualifications that are pursued.

Specialist professional qualifications

Qualified accountants are able to undertake a huge variety of roles both within and outside of the typical practice or industry roles (see Chapter 4 for more information) without undertaking further study. However, some specialised roles demand additional professional qualifications. Many accountants enjoy the opportunity to specialise in niche areas, not least because this also affords them the opportunity to study further.

Some individuals know from the outset that they would like to specialise in a particular area, and therefore take a direct entry route into their specialist field's qualification without undertaking an accountancy qualification first.

General study

Those accountants who do not wish to specialise in a distinct area often look for opportunities to advance their education so we will finish this chapter with a discussion of MBAs and continuing professional development.

Further professional qualifications

Insolvency

Have you ever wondered who the individuals are that try to rescue companies who have ended up in financial difficulty? In these challenging economic times, we are fast becoming familiar with headlines about companies placed into administration, receivership or liquidation. Insolvency Practitioners are the individuals dealing with these complex processes and, where possible, attempting to avoid insolvent liquidation by offering expert guidance.

Insolvency Practitioners (IPs) undertake varied and challenging work – they are licensed to advise on, and undertake appointments in,

all formal insolvency procedures including bankruptcy, liquidations, voluntary arrangements, receiverships and administrations.

In the UK insolvency is a regulated profession under the Insolvency Act 1986 and anyone who wishes to practise as an IP needs to pass the Joint Insolvency Examination Board (JIEB) exams prior to applying for an Insolvency Practitioner's Licence. Insolvency is a fairly exclusive professional field – there are a mere 2,500 UK IP licences in existence and fewer than 2,000 licence-holders actually practising as IPs.

Many IPs have a background in accountancy or law, and specialise in this challenging field after first pursuing their legal or accountancy qualifications. However, it is possible to pursue an insolvency career in the first instance.

Where a direct entry route is taken (ie not previously qualifying as an accountant), this usually starts with obtaining the Certificate of Proficiency in Insolvency (CPI). CPI equips the successful student with a sound knowledge of insolvency law and practice. It is a flexible, intermediate qualification that covers both corporate and personal insolvency. Once the CPI has been passed the candidate can gain membership of the Insolvency Practitioners Association (IPA). Membership entitles a member to describe themselves as an 'Insolvency Technician'. CPI training does not offer exemptions towards the Joint Insolvency Examination Board (JIEB) exams, which are mandatory for an Insolvency Practitioners Licence; however it provides a firm foundation for approaching them.

Qualified accountants (or lawyers) can go on to study for the prestigious JIEB exams, the set of professional examination papers which are mandatory for those who want to become a licensed insolvency practitioner. The three examinations are held once a year (usually in November) and each paper lasts 3.5 hours. It is possible to attempt all three papers at one sitting, though most candidates split the papers over two years. It is necessary to pass at least two JIEB papers during the same sitting in order to complete the qualification.

Once the JIEB exams have been passed, it is necessary to meet an authorising body's insolvency experience requirements in order to be fully qualified. The authorising body (or Recognised Professional Body (RPB)) in the UK is the Department for Business, Innovation & Skills (BIS).

IPs are sometimes referred to as 'turnaround specialists' and this field can certainly be an extremely rewarding career – see Chapter 4 for more information.

Taxation

The phrase 'tax specialist' encompasses a wide variety of professionals – HMRC inspectors; tax planners who devise schemes to mitigate taxes; tax compliance professionals who ensure their clients don't fall foul of the complex web of tax law; barristers who give opinions on complicated rules; teams who defend their clients in tax investigations, and even cross-border tax specialists who navigate the intricate world of tax treaties and double taxation agreements.

All of the mainstream accountancy routes involve the study of taxation to a greater or lesser extent and many qualified accountants have their interest sparked in this area as a result. Looking at the level of taxation studies in the four main accountancy qualifications, CIMA only looks at the basics of taxation, however ICAEW and ICAS routes cover tax in some significant detail (particularly corporation tax), and ACCA offers the opportunity to choose tax as a specialist advanced option paper (see Chapter 3 for more information on qualifications). Consequently it is possible to specialise in tax, particularly corporation tax, without undertaking further examinations once qualified as an accountant. No additional licence is required to undertake tax specialist work.

However, none of the mainstream accountancy qualifications furnish candidates with detailed knowledge about personal, capital and indirect taxes, nor do they purport to equip candidates with the skills necessary to utilise and interpret the vast tomes of tax legislation. As a result, where an individual has committed to a tax specialisation it is considered desirable, if not necessary, to undertake a specific tax qualification.

Qualified accountants (or lawyers) can go on to study for the Chartered Institute of Taxation qualification (Chartered Tax Adviser or CTA) or a candidate can take a direct entry approach into tax without undertaking accountancy or legal studies first by studying for membership of the Association of Taxation Technicians (ATT) then undertaking CTA.

In order to satisfy the examination requirements for membership of the ATT, students must complete two online assessments in Professional Responsibilities and Ethics and Law and pass three written examination papers. Two of the written papers are compulsory – Personal Taxation and Business Taxation and Accounting Principles, with the third chosen from: Business Compliance, Corporate Taxation, Inheritance Tax, Trusts and Estates, and Value Added Tax.

As well as passing the exams, students seeking certification as a registered taxation technician must be able to show that they have two years' relevant practical experience.

The Chartered Institute of Taxation's 'Chartered Tax Adviser' qualification is the premier specialised tax qualification available in the UK. It is held in the highest regard and those successful in the exams can use the designatory letters 'CTA' after their names and can usually expect a salary increase that reflects the associated prestige.

The examinations for the Chartered Institute of Taxation are widely recognised as some of the most demanding professional exams. Being a qualified accountant usually offers some exemptions (depending on the qualification undertaken), but assuming no exemptions, a CTA student is required to sit two online assessments (the same as those for ATT) and to undertake four three-hour written papers.

The written papers include two Advisory papers, one Awareness paper and one Application and interaction paper.

There are various versions of each paper, depending on whether the student wishes to pursue a specialism in personal tax, unincorporated business tax, corporate tax, inheritance tax and trusts or VAT and stamp duties.

Admission to membership is achieved by passing the Chartered Institute of Taxation's examinations and acquiring three years' relevant professional experience.

ATT and CTA exams are both held each year in May and November.

A career in tax is viewed by many accountants as a guarantee of varied and constantly changing work; refer to Chapter 4 for further information on a career in tax.

Treasury

Treasury management is all about handling the banking and funding requirements of a business, and managing its financial risk.

Treasury activities take place in companies (known as corporate treasury) but also in banks, financial institutions and in the public sector. Activities include raising and managing money, currency, commodity and interest rate risk, and often dealing with the related areas of insurance, pensions, taxation and property.

Most sizeable companies or organisations will have an employee with the title 'Treasurer' but even where no dedicated role exists; someone in the entity will almost certainly be undertaking the role as a part of their job. In a business which consists of a large group of international companies, a treasurer's role becomes essential.

The most widely recognised qualification in treasury management in the UK is the Association of Corporate Treasurers (ACT) qualification. Almost all of the FTSE 100 companies use ACT qualified treasury staff.

Many treasurers have an accountancy background and the ACT offers a fast-track route for qualified accountants who wish to gain the AMCT Diploma. However, it is possible to attempt the AMCT Diploma via direct entry (ie without a previous mainstream accountancy qualification).

To become a member of the ACT it is necessary to complete the AMCT Diploma or the MCT Advanced Diploma. The AMCT exams are taken in three stages. All papers are three-hour written examinations and exams are held twice a year, in April and October.

Stage one consists of four examination papers – Financial and Management Accounting, Economics and Statistical Analysis, Corporate Taxation and Business Law.

While direct-entry candidates must sit these four papers, qualified accountants are exempt from the stage one examination papers.

Stage two consists of one examination called the Certificate in International Treasury Management (CertITM). CertITM provides a broad understanding of the core elements of treasury; treasury, risk and corporate finance. A public finance version of this paper is also available.

Stage three consists of four examination papers, of which just two must be selected and passed. The four papers are: Cash Management, Risk Management, Corporate Finance and Funding, and Financial Maths and Modelling.

Treasury managers work in the heart of the company – the management of cash, funding and risk provides the foundations of a company and treasurers are able to see, first-hand, how the careful management of these areas can mean the difference between thriving, surviving and failure.

Company secretary

The company secretary position is one of great responsibility – a company secretary is closely involved with the board of directors and is used as an advisor to the board for legal and regulatory matters and risk management.

The specific duties of a company secretary and the extent of their role can vary. It depends upon the job description, which is determined by each entity in order to suit the size of the organisation and the industry in which it operates. Typical activities of the role, according to the

Institute of Chartered Secretaries and Administrators (ICSA), include: developing and managing strategies to ensure compliance with legal requirements; identifying areas for improved corporate governance; managing stakeholder communications and meetings; liaising with auditors, lawyers and tax advisors; and advising on issues essential to business performance, such as negotiation of contracts, finance, accounting, insurance and property.

Where an organisation is very large, and an individual would not be able to undertake all of the work, the role can be split with titles such as 'risk controller' 'assistant company secretary,' 'audit officer,' 'corporate administrator' and 'head of compliance / corporate governance.' As suggested by the title, company secretaries work for companies. However, a similar role is often required in not-for-profit organisations, charities and the NHS.

ICSA is the UK's leading professional body for company secretaries and with operations in Australia, Canada, Hong Kong, Malaysia, New Zealand, Singapore, South Africa and Zimbabwe, it aims to be a global voice on governance and regulatory issues.

In order to become ICSA qualified, it is necessary to succeed in the Chartered Secretaries Qualifying Scheme (CSQS) examinations and also to satisfy work experience and membership requirements. CSQS comprises two levels, each with four modules, as follows:

Level one

- Financial Reporting and Analysis

- Applied Business Law

- Corporate Law

- Corporate Governance *or* Health Service Governance

Level two

- Financial Decision Making

- Strategy in Practice

- Corporate Secretarial Practice

- Chartered Secretaries Case Study

It is possible to go into CSQS and the chartered secretary profession as a direct entry route, but many chartered secretaries have a background in accountancy or law, and a mainstream accountancy qualification affords significant exemptions from the examinations.

Upon passing the CSQS exams, the successful candidate is given graduate status and designated the title GradICSA. After completing the work experience requirements full membership status is given and the individual can use the designatory letters ACIS (Associate of the Chartered Institute of Secretaries) or FCIS (Fellow of the Chartered Institute of Secretaries) after their name.

Being a company secretary can be a highly rewarding career and is viewed by many as a fast-track route to a board-level role by those who have worked in the legal, accounting or corporate governance professions and want to take their career to the next step.

Financial services

The financial services industry is undeniably a major contributor to the UK and global economy, but it has also been under the press spotlight in recent years amid accusations of being instrumental in causing and aggravating the global economic downturn of recent years. In order to capitalise on the UK's strength in global financial services as well as attempt to prevent future catastrophe, financial services have become increasingly regulated, including requirements for proper training and qualification of staff working in the industry.

The financial services industry affects almost everyone and it has expanded in scope and complexity over the past 20 years. Included within its wide-ranging remit are all types of savings, pensions, insurance and mortgage products, and the industry operates in both wholesale (eg corporate banking) and retail (eg high street banking) sectors. It has been described as an industry which aims to provide a link between those needing money and those looking to invest.

Individuals who already have a mainstream accountancy qualification are undoubtedly already equipped with the knowledge and skills to undertake many roles within the financial services industry. However, many roles in financial services require individuals to have an in-depth understanding of the industry and the regulations that underpin it.

With increasing pressure being placed on those in the financial services industry to ensure the highest possible standards of professionalism, competence and ethics, financial services qualifications have gained momentum in recent years, and can certainly aid career progression.

The Chartered Institute for Securities & Investment (CISI) offers the most widely-recognised, specific financial services qualification. The CISI was formed in 1992 by London Stock Exchange practitioners and is a large and respected professional body for those who work in the securities and investment industry. The CISI is headquartered in the UK but also has recognition globally, having a presence in 88 other countries.

Direct entry into the CISI is possible, but a candidate who already holds a mainstream accountancy qualification is offered some significant exemptions. In particular, the ACCA has developed a partnership with the CISI with the express aim of giving ACCA members, who work or have an interest in the securities and investment industry, easy access to the CISI qualifications and membership, and guidance regarding the qualifications and / or exam papers most applicable to accountants working in, or wishing to move into, the securities and investments industry.

The CISI qualification process can appear complicated, not least because there is a significant array of choice over which modules to take, and four recognised streams (wholesale, wealth / retail, operations and specialists). However, in broad terms, there are four levels of examinations: foundation level, qualifying level, advanced level and postgraduate professional level. The CISI offers different levels of membership depending on the level of qualifications gained; there is a ladder of progression from 'Student' to 'Associate' to 'Member' and ultimately to 'Chartered Member' and 'Chartered Fellow'.

CISI modules

Foundation level

- Introduction to Investment or International Introduction to Investment

Qualifying level

- Level three Certificates in Commodity Derivatives, Derivatives, Financial Derivatives, Investment Management, Securities, International Investment Management, and Global Securities.

- Level four Diplomas in: Securities, Derivatives, Private Client Advice, and International Certificate in Wealth Management.

- The Investment Operations Certificate or IT in Investment Operations.

- Certificates in Financial Services for Directors, Corporate Finance, Islamic Finance, Risk in Financial Services, Combating Financial Crime, and Global Financial Compliance.

Advanced level

- Level five Diploma in Private Client Advice

- Advanced Certificates in Global Securities Operations or Operational Risk

Postgraduate professional level

- Diploma units in Bonds and Fixed Interest Markets, Financial Derivatives, Fund Management, or Regulation and Compliance

- CISI Diploma in Private Client Investment Advice and Management or CISI Masters in Wealth Management

- Diploma in Investment Operations

- Diploma in Investment Compliance

General study

MBA

Moving away from specialism (in the form of specialist professional qualifications) into more general qualifications; many accountants consider a Master's in Business Administration (MBA), seeing it as the perfect way to both further their academic studies and improve their career prospects as they become more senior within the organisations they work in.

An MBA is certainly a broad qualification. It is designed to widen the horizons of professionals in business by encouraging them to look at all of the major functions of a business, rather than focusing narrowly on their own area of specialism. An MBA is internationally recognised and seen as a way of supporting progress on a successful career path and developing managerial skill.

A candidate must have both studied and worked in order to be eligible to study for an MBA and neither of these requirements should be overlooked or underestimated – an MBA is very much designed as a postgraduate degree for experienced professionals. Students on an accredited MBA course usually bring five to ten years' postgraduate experience with them. Candidates who wish to study the topics covered in an MBA programme but who lack the necessary experience can look instead at a Master's in Business and Management.

The requirement for both previous study and significant experience means that cohorts of MBA candidates comprise highly successful and motivated individuals, and the networking opportunities afforded by studying for an MBA are frequently cited by candidates as one of the key advantages of studying for the qualification.

A large number of institutions hold accreditation to offer MBA programmes and it is possible to study via distance learning or part-time study at a number of universities across the globe. The level of

financial and time commitment involved is undoubtedly high, regardless of where the study is undertaken and a significant amount of time must therefore be invested in picking the institution and programme.

The benefits of an MBA are numerous, however. Research repeatedly shows that holders of MBAs are regularly paid higher salaries and have better job prospects than those working in the same field who do not hold the qualification. Most MBA holders work at senior management or at board level.

It is possible to take MBA studies to an even higher level by working towards a Doctorate in Business Administration (DBA). This is a research-based qualification where the candidate is seeking a solution to a management problem. It differs from a traditional PhD because there is still very much an emphasis on professional practice as well as academic knowledge, complementing the similar focus of the MBA. The DBA usually takes a minimum of four years to complete.

Continuing professional development

All qualified accountants are required by their institutes to maintain their professional knowledge after their accountancy qualification studies have ended, by undertaking continuing professional development (CPD) training. Each of the mainstream accountancy institutes designates the type of learning and minimum amount of time spent learning which is deemed to be sufficient to keep abreast of the required knowledge, and they have all invested time in approving and accrediting various training courses as relevant sources of CPD.

It is possible to view these CPD requirements as something of a chore and a box-ticking exercise where the qualified individual is forced to attend sufficient relevant courses to meet the requirements – this is indeed the mindset of many qualified individuals! However, this view is outdated and modern accountants are increasingly viewing CPD as a way to manage their own learning and development, and consequently their career progression.

CPD offers qualified accountants the opportunity to continue their studies and, even better; it affords them the chance to indulge in the study of relevant topics purely for the advancement of their knowledge without the pressure of an exam at the end of it!

Qualified accountants have a formal responsibility with their institute to keep their skills and knowledge up-to-date by actively managing, carefully designing and thoroughly recording their CPD programme, and it is possible to turn this enforced accountability into a positive opportunity to identify and set personal development goals and then chart progress towards achieving them. A well chosen CPD programme

undoubtedly enhances job satisfaction, and a well-charted CPD progress record which complements career objectives is a particularly useful document to produce at an annual performance appraisal or salary review meeting!

CPD courses are offered by a vast number of training providers. The key to choosing the right training is to verify that the provider is known for running well-regarded courses, and ensuring that the course offered fits well with your planned objectives.

Top tip

Before undertaking an accountancy qualification, make sure you find out what the annual CPD requirements of your chosen awarding body are. The amount of hours per year varies, as does the type of CPD, be it structured (such as attendance at a course) or unstructured (such as reading technical articles online). To find out more, have a look at the information provided by your chosen awarding body.

Chapter summary

Although it might seem unnecessary to undertake – or even consider! – further training once you have obtained your accountancy qualification, some training is always mandatory (such as continuing professional development) and should be viewed as a constructive way to enhance your skills. The opportunity to study further professional qualifications can greatly assist your career progression and salary (for example an MBA), or may simply be an area of interest for you to move into (for example ATT or CTA), so should not be disregarded.

Key points

- It is common for qualified accountants to undertake further studies.

- The choice of post-qualification study path will depend on your desired career or just personal choice.

- Post-qualification studies can result in higher salaries, faster career progression and greater job satisfaction.

Useful resources

Joint Insolvency Examination Board: www.jieb.co.uk

Insolvency exams advice: www.insolvencyexams.co.uk

Insolvency Practitioners Association: www.insolvency-practitioners.org.uk

Association of Taxation Technicians: www.att.org.uk

Chartered Institute of Taxation: www.tax.org.uk

Association of Corporate Treasurers: www.treasurers.org

Institute of Chartered Secretaries and Administrators: www.icsa.org.uk

Chartered Institute for Securities & Investment: www.cisi.org

Association of MBAs: www.mbaworld.com/mba

CIPD – CPD guidance: www.cipd.co.uk/cpd/aboutcpd/whatiscpd.htm

References

Association of Corporate Treasurers (2012) *AMCT Diploma in Treasury*. [Online] Available at: www.treasurers.org/qualifications/amct [Accessed 22 November 2012].

Association of MBAs (2012). [Online] Available at: www.mbaworld.com [Accessed 22 November 2012].

Association of Taxation Technicians (2012) *The Examinations*. [Online] Available at: www.att.org.uk/students/prospective/aboutexams [Accessed 22 November 2012].

Chartered Institute for Personnel and Development (2012) *What is CPD?* [Online] Available at: www.cipd.co.uk/cpd/aboutcpd/whatiscpd.htm [Accessed 22 November 2012].

Chartered Institute for Securities & Investment (2012) *Job Sectors and Profiles*. [Online] Available at: www.cisi.org/bookmark/genericform.aspx?form=29848780&url=Jobsectors [Accessed 22 November 2012].

Chartered Institute for Securities & Investment (2012) *Qualification and Programmes*. [Online] Available at: www.cisi.org/bookmark/genericform.aspx?form=29848780&URL=qualifications [Accessed 22 November 2012].

Chartered Institute of Taxation (2012) *Chartered Tax Adviser Prospectus and Syllabus*. [Online] Available at: www.tax.org.uk/students_qualifications/newctastudents/ctaprospectus [Accessed 22 November 2012].

Insolvency Practitioners Association (2012) *IPA – Putting Better Regulation into Practice*. [Online] Available at: www.insolvency-practitioners.org.uk [Accessed 22 November 2012].

Insolvencyexams.co.uk (2012) *Certificate of Proficiency in Insolvency Exam*. [Online] Available at: www.insolvencyexams.co.uk/?page_id=35 [Accessed 22 November 2012].

Institute of Chartered Secretaries and Administrators (2012) *How and Where to Study*. [Online] Available at: www.icsa.org.uk/join-us/study-to-be-a-chartered-secretary/how-and-where-to-study1#exams [Accessed 22 November 2012].

Institute of Chartered Secretaries and Administrators (2012) *What is a Chartered Secretary?* [Online] Available at: www.icsa.org.uk/join-us/study-to-be-a-chartered-secretary/what-is-a-chartered-secretary [Accessed 22 November 2012].

Joint Insolvency Exam Board (2012) *JIEB Exams – Information*. [Online] Available at: www.jieb.co.uk/jieb_exams [Accessed 22 November 2012].

Chapter 6

Finding work

Stuart Chandler

Introduction

In the introductory chapters of this book, we looked at the fact that as an accountant you can work almost anywhere – whether it is a hospital, a restaurant group or an oil company – the diversity and range of work is only limited to your preference.

Traditionally, an accountant's role is to work with financial information used by a business to make decisions and understand the current business environment. Many trainees therefore, will train with either a large professional services firm or a small / medium sized accountancy firm. Some trainee accountants are fortunate enough to obtain training contracts with numerous and varied small companies – for example a retail and hospitality group, an air conditioning repairs service or a recycling company (all of these are real-life examples of employers who send their staff to train with an international training company).

Definition

Training contract

In order to qualify as an accountant, trainees must both pass their exams and undertake a set amount of work experience; this is outlined in the **training contract**. It is separate from the employment contract between the member of staff and the employer.

A training contract is the piece of paper that many trainee accountants will sign upon acceptance of a place at a firm, and it outlines that the student must sit and pass their exams over a given period. It should clearly outline who will pay for exams (including the amount of resits), how much study leave will be given, minimum marks required in order to take the exams and so forth.

Bear in mind, though, that this is a legally binding contract, often containing a 'clawback clause' which states that, should you leave prior to filling your contractual duties, you may be liable to pay back any training costs incurred (either to date, or over the last 12 months). The point here is: read everything very carefully – if you do not read a contract, but sign it, it is still legally binding!

Employers

The 'Big Four'

The Big Four refers to the four largest professional services firms in the world: Deloitte, Ernst & Young, KPMG and PWC. These four companies are vast, with a global presence, a huge variety of career options and large numbers of staff.

The Big Four have a combined turnover of more than **US$103,000,000,000**! Globally, they employ more than 642,000 staff and have presence in nearly 160 countries. In the eyes of many, these are the premier places to undertake accountancy training, due to the international employment opportunities, and the financial backing and number of industries they deal with.

But it should be noted that while the Big Four are an excellent starting point to your accountancy career, they are not for everyone; working for a smaller practice (often with a wider variety of work) may suit you better, and is covered later on in more detail.

The Big Four offer accountancy positions to graduates or school leavers to train in audit, tax or corporate finance (see Chapter 4 for more information on each). They sponsor (pay) for their trainees to study with a recognised training provider, usually under ACCA, ICAEW or ICAS (see Chapter 3 for more information on qualifications). Tax trainees may also be required to sit the ATT and CTA exams either after, or instead of, an accountancy qualification.

> 'I decided upon PWC, as it was a high profile Big Four firm, which would provide me with some exciting work and development opportunities. I also enjoyed the thought of being able to obtain my ACA professional qualification and possible travel overseas later in my career.'

If the idea of larger professional services firms appeals to you, have a look at their websites:

- Deloitte: www.deloitte.com

- Ernst & Young: www.ey.com

- KPMG: www.kpmg.co.uk

- PWC: www.pwc.co.uk

Small and medium-sized entities

Small and medium-sized entities (SMEs) encompass a huge variety of industries: eg gardening, law, kitchen fitting, boat design, medicine or high street retail. This appears to be a disparate list without any binding element, however, if we consider the list, each of the above industries will need to employ, or use the services of, an accountant. You might not be directly employed as an accountant in a law firm or medical practice, but many SMEs need to have their financial statements audited, so you will gain exposure to these industries.

There is a wide range of medium-sized audit firms (commonly known as second tier firms), which offer the same services as the Big Four, but whose clients do not, for example, need the global presence offered by the Big Four. Consider HSBC, audited by KPMG, a vast company with offices globally which need to be audited. Compare this to the Co-operative Bank, which has a presence in the UK only. A second tier firm would be ideal as the auditor of this type of national organisation.

The second tier firms, such as BDO, Grant Thornton, RSM Tenon, Baker Tilly, Smith & Williamson, PKF, Moore Stephens, Mazars and Saffery Champness, offer accountancy training and financial support to thousands of accountancy students each year through their professional exams (ICAS, ICAEW and ACCA are commonly offered).

The difference between the second tier firms and the Big Four is often cited as the work: while a Big Four audit trainee may work on a very large client (such as HSBC or Lloyds TSB) for much of the year, only seeing fragments of the financial statements – which is understandable, given the size of these clients – trainees with second tier (and smaller firms) are able to see the entire audit process from planning to completion, dealing with key client staff and obtaining a solid grounding in how a business works.

Case study: You're the BDOnly one...

Sarah took a position as a trainee auditor with BDO, following completion of a Biological Sciences degree.

She felt that a second tier firm was well known, but not as daunting as a Big Four firm. It also sat better with her career goals, as the workload was more varied, and they were able to support her through her exams.

'I chose BDO as I preferred the work / life balance it offered me, compared to the Big Four firms. The development opportunities were important, as was the support and advice from both the firm and other students throughout my ACCA professional qualification.'

Small accountancy practices with one or two partners often offer an even greater variety of work than a second tier firm. With greater financial constraints, it is unlikely that these small practices will be able to employ a trainee tax consultant and a trainee auditor, meaning that your work will be highly varied. The greater responsibility from these firms is seen as a benefit which outweighs the (potential) lesser financial support.

As with any job, it really depends on your desired outcomes – if you want to travel with a large company, consider a Big Four firm; if you want to understand business better, consider a second tier firm, and if you would like to have a wide variety of work, a small firm would be suitable. There are, of course, many more advantages and disadvantages to all three options, but this will serve as a useful starting point for your decision.

Self employment

Self employment, or working for yourself, can take many different guises. You could start your own accountancy practice (either as a sole trader, or through formation of a limited company), or work as a consultant, going into businesses to assist with tax matters, financial reporting, compliance and other issues. The difference between the two is really to do with your clients – the work is not dissimilar. For example, as a consultant, you would go to a (usually larger) client's premises to work, whereas as a small practitioner, you are more likely to deal with smaller clients at your own office.

Many people aspire to run their own businesses at some stage during their lives, seeing it as a pinnacle of achievement. The benefits of having an accountancy qualification are that you will have a detailed understanding of how businesses are funded, what legal matters need to be considered and ultimately, what makes a business *tick*.

Unfortunately, self employment is not a realistic option for a trainee accountant, as most professional accountancy qualifications require various amounts of appropriate practical experience to be signed off by a member of staff within the training organisation. However, this does not mean that it is forever out of reach! Many start-up companies are begun and run by qualified accountants, following completion of their desired accounting qualification.

If the idea of having your own business (be it in accountancy or any area!) is appealing, refer to the government's business link website for more advice: www.businesslink.gov.uk.

Other opportunities

In order to qualify as an accountant, you will need to work with some facts and figures, as they are a large part of the professional exams, but also a requirement of the practical experience required for admission to membership by the various institutes. You can quickly choose to move away from working with numbers upon qualification, into another area of the business or a different industry.

The key with employment and qualification is: where do you want to work?

The chances are that the company and location you would like to move to will use the services of an accountant. Perhaps you would like to work as a tax consultant with Shell, BP or Esso? Maybe construction would suit you, so why not be a management accountant for Balfour Beatty or Mitie?

The list of companies, industries, jurisdictions and territories that require accountancy services is almost interminable, with the services of trainee and qualified staff proving invaluable to any modern company. The point is: draw up a list of industries, identify companies within that sector and contact them.

Top tip

If you have a good idea of the company or industry you would like to work in, contact the company directly and establish a rapport.

Send them a covering letter introducing yourself, attaching your CV and saying a couple of complimentary things about their company and why you want to work there (this should not be hard if you really want to work for them!).

Maintain that contact and they may be more likely to approach a friendly, open candidate with any positions, than to pay for advertising and recruitment.

Vacancies

Where to find work

If you want to find work in your local area, start with the local papers, magazines and job centres. These should also provide an insight in to the sorts of companies and industries that you will be able to work in – is it professional services? Manufacturing? Motoring? Retail? Hospitality? Financial services? – and help you decide if perhaps you need to cast your net wider.

If you know which company you would like to work with, then try going to their website and then establishing contact. It is worth noting that the Big Four firms have their own careers sections, as below:

- Deloitte: http://careers.deloitte.com

- Ernst & Young: www.ey.com/careers

- KPMG: www.kpmgcareers.co.uk

- PWC: www.pwc.co.uk/careers

If you don't know which company you want to work with, then there are some more general careers sites and services available, see the Useful resources section at the end of the chapter.

Chapter summary

Regardless of where you train, you will come out with the equivalent qualification to your peers, so try not to think of accountants only working as auditors, or as financial accountants; there are a wealth of accountancy jobs across a variety of industries and organisations – although don't forget that many training and travel opportunities are available with large accountancy firms. Finding a job and signing a training contract can seem daunting, but keep your eyes on the end goal: an internationally recognised qualification, allowing you to work in almost any industry.

Key points

- Remember – it is *your* career, therefore *your* decision!

- Do some background research on any possible employers.

- If you have no overriding desire to enter a specific industry; consider a professional services firm which will give you an excellent support network and insight into many industries.

- In the interview – don't be afraid to ask questions: you are interviewing them for a job, as much as they are interviewing you.

Useful resources

Careers advice

Accountancy Options: www.accountancy-options.co.uk

Business link: www.businesslink.gov.uk

Inside Careers: www.insidecareers.co.uk

The Accountancy Job: www.theaccountancyjob.com (jobs and advice)

Job vacancies

Accounting Jobs: www.accountingjobs.co.uk

Trainee Accountant Jobs: www.traineeaccountantjobs.co.uk

AccountancyAge Jobs: www.accountancyagejobs.co.uk

eFinancial Careers: www.efinancialcareers.co.uk

Hays Recruitment: www.hays.co.uk

Indeed job search: www.indeed.co.uk

Jobs Financial: www.jobsfinancial.com

Monster: www.monster.co.uk

Reed Recruitment: www.reed.co.uk

The Big Four

Deloitte: www.deloitte.com

Ernst & Young: www.ey.com

KPMG: www.kpmg.co.uk

PWC: www.pwc.co.uk

References

HSBC (2011) *HSBC Holdings plc Annual Report and Accounts 2011.* [Online] Available at: http://www.hsbc.com/1/PA_esf-ca-app-content/content/assets/investor_relations/hsbc2011ara0.pdf [Accessed 22 November 2012].

ICAEW (2012) *ACA Training Agreements.* [Online] Available at: www.icaew.com/en/qualifications-and-programmes/aca/aca-employers/aca-training-agreements [Accessed 22 November 2012].

Wikijob (2011) *Training Contract.* [Online] Available at: www.wikijob.co.uk/wiki/training-contract [Accessed 22 November 2012].

Wikipedia (2012) *Big Four Audit Firms.* [Online] Available at: http://en.wikipedia.org/wiki/Big_Four_(audit_firms) [Accessed 22 November 2012].

Chapter 7

Working abroad

Stuart Chandler

Introduction

One of the many highlights of becoming an accountant is that you can choose to work anywhere – not just with regard to industry but location. Chapter 4 assessed various work options for accountants, from the point of view of a trainee. Once qualified, the world of work opens up further still.

In this chapter we consider where you might work, as well as whether your new qualification – be it from CIMA, ACCA, AAT, CAI, ICAS or ICAEW – will be recognised overseas.

Opportunities abroad

Working overseas within a large company is a clear benefit of working with an international organisation, whether with a bank or an audit firm. The differing cultures will help your management style, your perspective and putting all that to one side – it should be a fun experience!

> 'Working and living in Holland was very interesting for a number of reasons, working abroad being the most obvious but it was also my first time being solely responsible for managing a team of people... I also loved the Dutch people and their approach to life!'

It is not necessary to undertake a training programme with an international company just to exploit potential overseas opportunities; an accountancy qualification will help you to travel and work independently with employers overseas.

Case study: Big Four – international opportunities

Alex is currently on secondment with a Big Four audit firm in Australia.

How did you find a job overseas?

'One of the advantages of working with a large firm is the opportunity to move around the globe relatively easily. I raised the idea of working overseas with my coach and from there the ball started to roll. With a large firm, one of the hardest decisions is where to choose to go in the first place – although my move was at the time of an economic downturn so there were fewer options than usual. All overseas opportunities are advertised on a global firm website and from this I made my selection after considering factors like location (obviously, but included thoughts on culture, language and even food!), work opportunities and relevance to my long term career goals. Once I made my decision the firm made the move happen and it was a very easy process, heavily supported and facilitated by the firm's network and internal global mobility department.'

Where did you decide to work and why?

'I have always worked in a predominately financial services environment and with my move being just temporary I didn't want to venture away from this. I can remember in my first interview over ten years ago discussing the opportunities of working overseas and the benefits of working for a large firm, so I'm glad I finally made use of this benefit and moved to Sydney with the same firm. This has many advantages: familiarity, the same computer systems, quality infrastructure and like-minded colleagues.

As for choosing Sydney, it ticked all the boxes for me personally and professionally.'

How did work overseas differ from your home working environment?

'I have two variables to consider here, one being overseas and the other being a move from a small office to a very large office – so in terms of pinning the differences down to each variable, it is quite hard. On reflection, I think the move from a small office of 100 to a large office of 6,000+ has been the biggest change for me. The working environment has been somewhat tougher in terms of demands and hours, but this is countered by the abundance of amazing weekend activities falling right on my doorstep. Work hard, play hard seems to be a consistent message!'

Did you have to undertake any conversion exams for your qualifications?

'No, none were needed with my ICAEW qualification.'

According to the Financial Reporting Council's *Key Facts and Trends in the Accountancy Profession* June 2011 report, there were nearly 120,000 qualified accountants (from the seven qualifying bodies surveyed in the UK: ACCA, CIMA, CIPFA, ICAEW, CAI, ICAS and AIA) working outside of the UK.

Clearly, there will be benefits to your professional development and personal growth to working overseas. However, this is only possible if your qualification is actually recognised, thus enabling you to work as an accountant. Read on for more information on the recognition of your desired or current qualification.

Recognition of qualifications

Another benefit of qualifying as an accountant, as opposed to say, a lawyer, is that your qualification may be recognised overseas. The emergence and continued convergence of International Financial Reporting Standards, International Standards on Auditing and International Accounting Standards has led to the professional skills being transferable.

So the question is: if you study for an accountancy qualification, will your qualification be recognised overseas?

See the below table for the span of recognition:

Qualification or awarding body	Area of recognition*
ACCA	International
ACA (from ICAEW)	International
CA (from ICAS)	International
ACA (from CAI)	International
CIMA	International
AAT	International
CAT (from ACCA)	International
CIPFA	International

*Always confirm with the awarding institute for the specific country's requirements before relocating overseas.

Table 7.1: Recognition of qualifications overseas

Top tip

If you are an overseas accountant who would like to come to the United Kingdom, and are unsure whether your qualifications will apply in the UK, try going to www.naric.org.uk and applying for a personal statement of comparability.

Alternatively, check www.globalaccountingalliance.com for the name of your awarding institute, and you will be able to establish whether or not you have a reciprocal membership agreement.

Chapter summary

Being able to transfer and work overseas is a clear benefit of an accountancy qualification, allowing you incredible opportunities. The development of your skills and knowledge as an accountant who has worked overseas means you can be better prepared for progression to management, as you have demonstrated an ability to adapt. In the midst of it all though, don't forget that it should be an exciting and enjoyable experience!

Key points

- Working overseas is a great way to travel the world and get paid!

- Having international experience on your CV is a good signal to employers that you are able to work in different environments.

- Your qualification *should* be recognised overseas, but always check with the awarding body before you go, as it can be country-specific.

Useful resources

National Agency for Information on Recognition of Qualifications: www.naric.org.uk

Global Accounting Alliance: www.globalaccountingalliance.com

Association of Chartered Certified Accountants: www.accaglobal.com

Chartered Institute of Management Accountants: www.cimaglobal.com

Chartered Institute of Public Finance and Accountancy: www.cipfa.org.uk

Institute of Chartered Accountants in England and Wales: www.icaew.com

Chartered Accountants Ireland: www.charteredaccountants.ie

Institute of Chartered Accountants in Scotland: www.icas.org.uk

Association of International Accountants: www.aiaworldwide.com

References

AAT (2012) *What We Do*. [Online] Available at: www.aat.org.uk/about-aat/what-we-do [Accessed 22 November 2012].

ACCA (2012) *About Us*. [Online] Available at: www.accaglobal.com/en/discover/about.html [Accessed 22 November 2012].

CAI (2012) *Chartered Accountants Ireland Global*. [Online] Available at: www.charteredaccountants.ie/General/About-Us/Chartered-Accountants-Ireland-Global [Accessed 22 November 2012].

CIMA (2012) *About Us*. [Online] Available at: www.cimaglobal.com/About-us/ [Accessed 22 November 2012].

CIPFA (2012) *About CIPFA*. [Online] Available at: www.cipfa.org/About-CIPFA [Accessed 22 November 2012].

Financial Reporting Council, Public Oversight Body (2011) *Key Facts & Trends Reports, 2011*. [Online] Available at: www.frc.org.uk/getattachment/1b7baf93-3be3-4fba-b4c1-dec90874b23d/Key-Facts-and-Trends-in-the-Accountancy-Profession-27-June-2011.aspx [Accessed 22 November 2012].

ICAEW (2012) *Who We Are*. [Online] Available at: www.icaew.com/en/about-icaew/who-we-are [Accessed 22 November 2012].

ICAS (2012) *What We Do*. [Online] Availabe at: http://icas.org.uk/What_we_do.aspx [Accessed 22 November 2012].

Chapter 8

Case studies

Case study 1

Naomi is a corporate tax director at a top 25 accountancy firm.

What qualifications did you have before you moved into accountancy?

'A levels.'

What made you decide on accountancy?

'I enjoyed Maths A level and thought I would enjoy a career using those numerical skills; I also wanted to take advantage of the great training scheme offered by BDO to school leavers which, I felt, would give me a head start in my career over those going to university to do a degree.'

What qualification did you undertake and why?

'As part of the training scheme with BDO I studied for the Association of Accounting Technicians (AAT) exams followed by the Institute of Chartered Accountants in England & Wales (ICAEW) exams. After finishing my ICAEW qualification, I was working in general practice and really enjoyed the tax work I did, so decided to study for my Chartered Tax Advisor (CTA) exams.'

Where have you worked, and what have you done?

'I started out in BDO's audit department, followed by time at a small practice preparing VAT returns and payroll, as well as providing accounting and tax services for small businesses and charities. After that, I moved to Ernst & Young as a tax manager and now Wilkins Kennedy as director of corporate tax planning.'

What do you do now, and what is a typical day?

'As with many jobs in accountancy, there is not really a typical day. In my role, I am responsible for corporate tax planning; I have a small team working with me and we help our clients, who are mainly owner-managed businesses, to plan their tax affairs. I get involved with a lot of enquiries about the Enterprise Investment Scheme, looking at succession planning within a business and the purchase of a company's own shares as well as advice on Research and Development tax credits. We spend time getting to know our clients and their needs, sitting down with them to suggest ways they can plan and organise their business to reduce their tax bill.

I spend quite a lot of time looking at tax legislation, considering how it applies to my clients and also responding to Her Majesty's Revenue and Customs queries (the tax authority in the UK). I do enjoy winning an argument with Her Majesty's Revenue and Customs! One of the most satisfying things I have done in my career to date is get agreement from them on the tax status of one of my clients – it took two years but I won the row, which was worth £1,800,000 in tax to my client!

I occasionally prepare tax computations for my clients, if they are keen that one person provides all their tax services, but it is not a part of the job I enjoy as much; I prefer using my problem-solving skills in tax planning.'

What does the future hold?

'I really enjoy my job so I'm looking to build the team that I have working with me and spend more time on winning new business. I hope to soon get promoted to partner in the firm.'

Case study 2

Ben works as a corporate recovery specialist in Sydney.

What qualifications did you have before you moved into accountancy?

'Prior to commencing my studies in accounting I had recently completed the Higher School Certificate (known as the HSC). This is the final set of exams in New South Wales, Australia for high school students and the primary requirement to be accepted into tertiary education in Australia.'

What made you decide on accountancy?

'While I was pursuing my undergraduate degree, a Bachelor of Business, global corporate failures were very topical in Australia. We had Australian Stock Exchange (ASX) listed companies such as HIH Insurance, One-Tel and Ansett Airlines all hitting the front page of the newspapers as being the biggest corporate disasters in Australian history. This appeared to be a very exciting area of the accounting discipline and one in which I could develop my career.

I was lucky enough to secure a junior role in an accounting firm which specialised in insolvency, restructuring and turnaround advisory. From this point on I majored in Accounting and worked part-time with an accounting firm until the completion of my studies, where I continued full-time.'

What qualification did you undertake and why?

'I studied the Certified Practising Accountants (CPA) programme which is administered by CPA Australia. It provided me with a diverse range of courses to assist me in my work while also being globally recognised, enabling me to travel the world and work as a qualified accountant.'

Where have you worked, and what have you done?

'I started out in Sydney, working for two small accounting firms which specialised in formal insolvency appointments / procedures such as administrations and deeds of company arrangement.

Following completion of my CPA and with three years' experience under my belt I moved over to the United Kingdom and worked with both Moore Stephens LLP and Grant Thornton UK LLP in London. With Moore Stephens LLP I was primarily involved in large scale administrations and liquidations. At Grant Thornton UK LLP I was part of the Healthcare Financial Advisory Services team which provided advisory services to NHS organisations, particularly NHS Trusts which are in deficit.

Upon my return to Australia I continued working with Grant Thornton, specialising in providing independent business reviews to large clients, including international banks. I am now back with the original firm I commenced my career with working in administrations and liquidations.'

What do you do now, and what is a typical day?

'Now I am managing an insolvency team of four people within a small practice which specialises in administrations and liquidations.

The beauty about my work is that I never have days that are the same. One day I could be co-ordinating a sale of business for an ASX listed company, the next day I could be establishing trading control procedures for a manufacturing company and trading the business through a restructuring process. Each day you find yourself in a new situation and each situation is a learning experience regardless of how long you have worked in accountancy.'

What does the future hold?

'With the global financial crisis still lingering in the air, insolvency and corporate recovery specialists remain in demand.

This year I will study the Insolvency Practitioners Association of Australia (IPAA) course which will enable to me to apply for my 'ticket' as a registered liquidator so that I can take appointments on administrations and liquidations. From there I will hopefully progress towards partnership in the practice...'

Case study 3

Sadie is a professional tutor at an international training organisation in Leeds.

What qualifications did you have before you moved into accountancy?

'I had GCSEs and A levels, after which I undertook a degree in Japanese Studies at Durham University.'

Why made you decide on accountancy?

'It was an absolute accident! I wanted to use my Japanese in my career and was offered a position at Arthur Andersen (which subsequently became Deloitte) in their Japanese human capital team, providing UK tax advice to Japanese expatriates in the UK. I heard the words: 'London,' 'Japanese' and 'study' and thought it sounded right up my street without giving the accountancy angle any thought whatsoever!'

What qualification did you undertake and why?

'I started out with Association of Taxation Technicians (ATT), then Chartered Institute of Taxation (CTA) – I undertook these because they were a compulsory part of my training contract with Deloitte, and essential in order for me to be able to do my job.

A few years later I took the Certified Accounting Technician (CAT) and I'm now three exams away from being a member of the Association of Chartered and Certified Accountants (ACCA). I undertook these two qualifications because I wanted to be broader in my qualifications, rather than specialised in tax and because they give me a wider spectrum of career opportunities.'

Where have you worked, and what have you done?

'My first role was with Arthur Andersen in London. I was on their graduate training scheme, working in the area of Japanese expatriate taxation. After qualifying, I moved to Deloitte and Walbrook Trust in Guernsey, working in the area of offshore trust taxation and tax planning for UK residents. I then moved to work with Ernst & Young, working in the area of UK non-domiciliaries and tax planning for non-domiciles and non-residents using offshore trusts, companies and other vehicles.

Following Ernst & Young I moved out of practice to work with BPP Professional Education in Guernsey, where I tutored tax, law, audit and financial accounting as well as being the ACCA programme manager. The decision was then made to move back to the UK, where I worked with Deloitte in Leeds in the area of owner-managed business taxation.'

What do you do now, and what is a typical day?

'I now work for BPP Professional Education in Leeds, tutoring tax, law, audit and financial accounting for professional examinations.

My average day starts off with a dash to the train station, where I jump on the 7:28 am train and get to our Leeds office just before 8:00 am. For the next 45 minutes I answer emails from students and then head into class. Classes run from 9:00 am until 4:15 pm – while the students take regular breaks, the tutor is normally answering questions for most of those, coupled with the fact that all professional qualification courses are time-pressured; it is a pretty intense day!

My subjects range from fairly straightforward (such as the foundation-level accounting papers) up to absolute rocket science (CTA papers!) and each presents its own challenges. The harder subjects leave you feeling completely exhausted but quite elated at having not only got through it in one piece, but also having made something a little less terrifying for your grateful and trusting students. The foundation level courses can be exhilarating if you keep the class entertained, build up a rapport and get a bit of banter going.

At 4:15 pm I wave goodbye to the students and head back into the office, normally to answer a few more emails, print notes and schedules and deal with admin such as student reports. Then I head home and usually prepare my notes for a couple of hours.

I get massive amounts of satisfaction from my job – I really can't begin to express how much I enjoy teaching, I love feeling like I understand my subjects better and better. Some tutors like to specialise in one or two topics and enjoy being the 'grand master' of that paper. While I enjoy an element of that, I thrive on the challenge of teaching a wide range of subjects and try to take on a new paper as often as is feasible.'

What does the future hold?

'I'd like to continue improving at teaching my subjects, and look forward to taking on new subjects including degree lecturing. I am still studying myself and would like to continue to study for new qualifications. Career progression at BPP can take many guises and I'm very attracted to some of the managerial responsibilities – watch this space!'

Case study 4

Gary runs his own tax and consulting firms, and is a freelance tutor in Manchester.

What qualifications did you have before you moved into accountancy?

I chose my O level and A level subjects based on what I liked and what I thought I was good at, but had no real regard for what I wanted to be in the future. Fortunately, I ended up with a good mix of O levels but ended up choosing History, Sociology and Politics as my A levels – don't ask me why as I dislike all three!'

What made you decide on accountancy?

'After A levels I wanted to earn some money and was not interested in getting a degree (no one in my family had a degree, so it was not really mentioned); as I was more 'white collar' than 'blue collar' (my Dad was in insurance), I joined NatWest as an A level trainee. I soon realised two things: first, banking was not for me, and second, it would take years to work through the corporate hierarchy without a degree and / or a professional qualification.

I lasted 12 months with NatWest but in that time had started some banking exams and accountancy was one of the subjects I studied. Not only did I like the idea of working with money, I started to see that accountants earned a decent salary, certainly more than I could have earned in the bank! Decision made, I left the bank and enrolled on an accounting and finance degree.'

What qualification did you undertake and why?

'After I graduated, I had a further choice to make: should I go into audit or industry? For me the latter was the only real option. I wanted to work in industry for a real business, and so by default (at that time), the CIMA qualification was the chosen route in industry. My degree gave me certain exemptions and it was possible to be professionally qualified within two years… I just needed a job!'

Where have you worked, and what have you done?

'In life, there are certain pivotal points when you look back and I can identify two in terms of my career. The first was being accepted on a graduate training scheme with British Nuclear Fuels (BNFL). This gave me a job with more money than I could spend, day release for two years to study for my CIMA qualification, and a structured internal training programme covering all financial areas of the business.

After becoming exam qualified with BNFL I moved to be a management accountant with a small software company. They were a niche player in the electronic banking world and were subsequently acquired by a large American company. My role then expanded and I started to travel and work in the US.

My second pivotal point then occurred: the Chief Financial Officer of the parent company, Marty Goldstein, visited the UK and after spending some time with me, decided to appoint me as the UK Finance Director (FD). It should be noted that this broke all HR protocol at the time, but in that decision, he elevated me to a senior position, giving me a real push up the corporate ladder.

From a corporate perspective, I never looked back as my career progressed with the US parent, ultimately becoming their International FD, when they started to venture into other territories. We floated on NASDAQ as eFunds Corporation, and became the largest third party outsourcer in India covering call centres, software development and back office processing. My time was spent between Arizona, Sydney, Delhi and Runcorn – I was living the dream!

However, over time, I started to tire of the travel and what I refer to as 'the corporate merry-go-round' where senior people come into organisations, change things, and then move on (with hefty payoffs!). The issue is that the rest of the organisation are left to pick up the pieces and try to carry on. I wanted a change, and thought that with my experience, knowledge and qualification that I could easily go independent and try working as a consultant – how wrong was I?!

The independent life was tough – I needed to market myself, find business, establish relationships, deal with all the administration and then try to collect my money! The corporate world of a big salary, good benefits, and support staff was now looking really good. I persevered and spent several years working as a consultant for larger clients; an interim FD for small-and medium-sized clients; a freelance tutor for the CIMA qualification and roles on several boards – before deciding that I wanted to develop my own business.

I started with Numerological, which specialises in Spanish tax for UK people with property in Spain, dealing with all possible tax situations – purchase, rental, sale, inheritance – so everything can be dealt with from the UK. I have clients across the UK covering properties across the whole of Spain. The second business is Strategy Office, borne out of my time working with and on boards of directors. I developed a methodology and process, which if followed, can significantly increase the probability that a company's strategy will be understood and implemented successfully.'

What do you do now, and what is a typical day?

'My time now is spent between my businesses and working as a freelance tutor.

Fortunately for me I don't really have a typical day! It really depends on what 'hat' I am wearing: it could be helping a senior executive team to develop a strategy or helping them review their strategy on a page, identifying appropriate actions and responsibilities; it could be meeting up with Spanish property owners to discuss and explain their individual tax situation in Spain; or it could be teaching degree students various subjects (most recently Quantitative Techniques, Business Communications and Managerial Finance!).'

What does the future hold?

'Having experienced corporate life and self-employed life, the latter is where I will now stay – I would now find it very hard to work for someone and within the constraints of an organisational structure.

I would like to continue to develop my businesses, but will also have an eye out for new business opportunities (there have been many ideas that have failed!) and also continue to teach; working with students and young professionals can be very interesting, as you see different perspectives and new ways of working, as well as being both rewarding and fun.

The real beauty of the independent professional lifestyle is that, once established, you can really start to choose the work that you like and the people you like working with, it therefore no longer becomes work and instead is just the way you live your life. Long may it continue!'

Case study 5

Rachel is managing director for a hospitality group.

What qualifications did you have before you moved into accountancy?

A levels, followed by a degree in Accounting and Finance from Oxford Brookes.

What made you decide on accountancy?

I could see that with an accountancy qualification, I would be able to travel and have significant opportunities available to me wherever I chose to go...I was also too short sighted to be a pilot!

What qualification did you undertake and why?

I undertook the ACA qualification from the Institute of Chartered Accountants in England and Wales, as I felt it was the preferred qualification for someone in practice. It was also well recognised internationally, in the event that I wanted to work overseas.

Where have you worked, and what have you done?

I started out on the graduate training programme with PWC, as a trainee in their tax department. I was responsible for tax compliance, negotiations with the tax office regarding client affairs and tax planning for corporations and individuals.

After qualifying, I moved to KPMG as a manager in their tax department, where I took on responsibility for managing, recruiting and developing a team, as well as the day-to-day review of junior's work.

Following this, I moved to a retail group, as their finance director. I was responsible for business development, group operations and financial reporting – something of a shift from tax work, but it was hugely challenging and enjoyable.

What do you do now, and what is a typical day?

I have recently moved to a restaurant group, as managing director. I'm responsible for the ongoing success of the group, and its development and growth; I deal with staff at all levels of the business, oversee the finance team and manage external relationships with suppliers/service providers (eg lawyers, banks), all the while looking out for, and evaluating, potential opportunities for growth.

There isn't really a typical day for me – this industry is a fast, hectic one where things can change in an instant. I invariably head to the office in the morning to catch up on email, discuss current performance with the finance team and clear off any pressing issues. I then try to meet with the manager at each restaurant at least once a week for a catch up. I also meet with the business's shareholders on a regular basis – but all of this can disappear out of the window in a few minutes; a power cut can be disastrous in the middle of lunch service and needs all hands on deck to deal with and resolve!

What does the future hold?

I am lucky enough to thoroughly enjoy my job – so I hope to continue to grow the business and expand, whether by hiring more staff or acquiring other sites. I also want to follow my original dream of qualifying as a private pilot in case the day job doesn't last..!

Glossary

Abbreviations

Abbreviation	Definition
AAPA	Association of Authorised Public Accountants
AAT	Association of Accounting Technicians
ACA	Association of Chartered Accountants (members of ICAEW or CAI)
ACCA	Association of Chartered Certified Accountants
ACT	Association of Corporate Treasurers
AIA	Association of International Accountants
ASB	Accounting Standards Body
ASX	Australian Stock Exchange
ATI	Accounting Technicians Ireland
ATT	Association of Taxation Technicians
CA	Chartered Accountant (member of ICAS)
CAI	Chartered Accountants Ireland
CAT	Certified Accounting Technician
CCAB	Consultative Committee of Accountancy Bodies
CEO	Chief Executive Officer
CFO	Chief Financial Officer
CIMA	Chartered Institute of Management Accountants
CIOT	Chartered Institute Of Taxation
CIPFA	Chartered Institute of Public Finance & Accountancy
CISI	Chartered Institute for Securities & Investment
CMI	Chartered Management Institute
CPA	Certified Public Accountant
CPI	Certificate of Proficiency in Insolvency
CSR	Corporate Social Responsibility
CTA	Chartered Tax Advisor (member of CIOT)

Abbreviation	Definition
FASB	Financial Accounting Standards Board
FD	Finance Director
FIA	Foundations In Accountancy
FRC	Financial Reporting Council
FSA	Financial Services Authority
FTSE	Financial Times Stock Exchange
HMRC	Her Majesty's Revenue & Customs
IASB	International Accounting Standards Board
ICAEW	Institute of Chartered Accountants in England and Wales
ICAS	Institute of Chartered Accountants in Scotland
ICSA	Institute of Chartered Secretaries and Administrators
IFAC	International Federation of Accountants
IFRS	International Financial Reporting Standards
IPAA	Insolvency Practitioners Association of Australia
JIEB	Joint Insolvency Examination Board
LLC	Limited Liability Company
LLP	Limited Liability Partnership
LSE	London Stock Exchange
LTD	Limited Company
MBA	Masters in Business Administration
MD	Managing Director
PLC	Public Limited Company
POB	Public Oversight Board
SME	Small-or medium-sized entity
UK GAAP	United Kingdom Generally Accepted Accounting Practice

Terms

Term	Definition
Accounts	See 'Financial statements'.
Assets	The items owned by a company, eg cash, buildings or vehicles.
Audit	The independent examination of historic financial information, undertaken by an independent, external professional.
Awarding bodies	Refers to the institutes that award accountancy qualifications: AAT, ACCA, CAI, CIMA, CIPFA, ICAEW and ICAS.
Balance sheet	Statement in the financial statements showing the assets, liabilities and shares of a company. Also referred to as the statement of financial position.
Big Four	The largest professional services providers in the world: Deloitte, Ernst & Young, KPMG and PWC.
Budget	The financial plan of a business; sets out how much money a business expects to make (income), how much it expects to spend (expenses) over the course of a financial year.
Controls	The systems of reviews and checks in place to prevent, detect and correct any theft, errors or fraud in a company.
Due diligence	Process by which a company (the acquirer) looking to invest or buy another company (the target), tries to understand what assets or liabilities the target has, and whether (or not) it is worth the acquirer investing.
Equity	See 'Shares'.
Expenses	Outflows of money from a business, such as payment of rent, electricity or salaries.

Term	Definition
External audit	External audit is the independent examination of historical financial information (most commonly the annual financial statements), whereby the auditor will consider what the financial statements are stating and compare this to the underlying records, concluding by stating an opinion on the financial statements.
Financial accountant	Prepares the financial statements of a company.
Financial Services Authority	The UK's finance industry regulator.
Financial statements	Summary of a company's financial records; financial statements show what a company owns (assets), what it owes (liabilities); how it has made money (income) and what it has spent money on (expenses). Also known as the accounts.
Financial year	Period for which accounts of a company are prepared, usually 12 months in duration, such as 1 January 2012 – 31 December 2012.
Income	Sources of incoming funds for a company, such as sales of cars / houses / MP3 players, bank interest received or dividends received.
Income statement	See 'Profit & loss report'.
Internal audit	Members of the internal audit team are employees who review the internal processes and controls of their company.
Internal control	See 'Controls'.
Liabilities	What is owed by a company, such as an overdraft with the bank, a mortgage on a property or unpaid expenses.
Management accountant	Prepares the management accounts of a company.

Term	Definition
Management accounts	Highly detailed, internal information, used by managers to budget, plan production and understand the costs of a company.
Profit & loss report	Statement in the financial statements showing the income and expenses of a company (if there is more income than expense, the company makes a profit; if there is more expense than income, the company makes a loss). Also called the income statement.
Retail Distribution Review	Sets out minimum standards to be held by investment professionals.
Shares	Unit of ownership of a company; entitles the holder to a share of the company's profits, losses, assets or liabilities. Also known as equity.
Statement of financial position	See 'Balance sheet'.
Training contract	A training contract is what many trainee accountants will sign upon acceptance of employment and it outlines that the student must sit and pass their exams over a given period.

Index